A Path of Wisdom

Lama Jigme Rinpoche

A Path of Wisdom

Lama Jigme Rinpoche

*Edited by Sylvia Wong
and Audrey Desserrières*

A Path of Wisdom
© Rabsel Éditions, France, 2012

ISBN 978-2-9537216-5-2

Contents

A Path of Wisdom is based on the original series of lectures of the same name given from 1997 to 1999 in Dhagpo Kagyu Ling by Lama Jigme Rinpoche who also added further explanations for this book.

Introduction

To truly benefit from any Buddhist practice, we seek to understand the essential points at the heart of the Buddha's teachings. They encapsulate the profound meanings the Buddha taught and are therefore critical and indispensable for the accomplishment of the Buddhist path. This book presents a way of Buddhist practice with applications in everyday life. We pay close attention to the precise meanings underlying the essential points, and methods. We try to understand correctly the meaning of Refuge, prayer, the enlightened attitude, the connection with the spiritual friend, the different practices, and meditation. *The Jewel Ornament of Liberation*[1] by Gampopa[2] (1079-1153) is an excellent source of reference for these topics. Once we have the

---

[1] Gampopa, *The Jewel Ornament of Liberation, The Wish-fulfilling Gem of the Noble Teachings*, Snow Lion, Ithaca, 1998.

[2] One of the founding masters of the Kagyü school of Tibetan Buddhism.

proper understanding, we integrate it into our practice and daily life. In this way, we will develop and deepen our knowledge of how we function, and recognize what is meaningful in our lives.

Practitioners vary in capacity depending on their inner understanding of the Dharma, the Buddha's teachings. In general, the very experienced practitioners, who have already grasped the essential points of the Dharma, know exactly what is required to achieve the goal of enlightenment. The less experienced can improve their understanding by listening and then reflecting carefully on the essential points. Through their practice, the meaning will become clearer, which will in turn enhance further progress on the path. As for beginners who have not yet started to practice, the essential points may be difficult to appreciate. Nevertheless, it is still beneficial to try to comprehend as much as possible rather than simply rejecting them. The understanding thus gained can afford some direction and guidance which may gradually lead to Dharma practice. Even for someone who does not wish to practice, some understanding of the essential points can still prove useful in everyday life.

The Buddha taught the Dharma to liberate all living beings from suffering, and to realize mind's true nature which will culminate in enlightenment. The vast and profound teachings and methods place us squarely on the path so we can go step by step staying focused and in the right direction. Otherwise, enlightenment is

beyond our reach like walking in the desert –
we can keep going but there is no end in sight.
The teachings often sound simple and easy to
understand, but to really get the gist of the
Dharma requires training and regular application. Like the desert, there is much more than
what meets the eye.

Whenever we listen to the teachings, we may
not get the exact meaning right away. Very
often, we are not even aware of the gaps in our
understanding. Because we are not familiar with
what is being explained, we don't feel that something is missing. This is natural. We tend to hear
and catch what we can understand thinking that
we understand it all. It is good to be aware that
this can happen.

Whether we can grasp the meaning of the
Dharma very much depends on our understanding.
When we do, it will inevitably translate into a
stronger commitment towards greater clarity of
mind ultimately leading to enlightenment itself.
In general, people new to Buddhism attend the
teachings and go away feeling that they have
learnt the methods. Rather than taking the time
to recognize the underlying meanings, they may
get caught up in the technicalities of the practices.
As a result, their expectations are neither right
nor realistic so that little improvements or positive effects go unnoticed even when they are
there. They feel enlightenment unattainable or
too far removed from their current situation.
Feeling discouraged, they give up. This is why
we must take the time to first understand the
meanings and what to expect from the teachings.

Seasoned practitioners, on the other hand, understand the essence of the teachings and appreciate the gradual improvements, which benefit their daily lives. They are confident that the Dharma methods are effective while fully appreciating the enormity of their undertaking. They know that nobody can give them enlightenment. The challenge is far different than passing examinations and graduating with an academic degree. Enlightenment has to come from one's own mind through one's own practice. A seasoned practitioner also appreciates the value of any progress made, which yields a clearer and more peaceful mind – a mind where there is more understanding, less suffering, and the emotions are less disturbing and intense. That mind can also understand the conditions in which we are trapped and recognizes the opportunity to limitlessly develop the inner potential of love and compassion. By engaging in altruistic actions, merits are accumulated to strengthen and support one's practice and daily life. All these factors are interdependent and they advance the practitioner further on the path to enlightenment.

The essential points of the Dharma are presented in this book to enable you to really connect to the meaning of the Dharma. We will examine some words specific to Tibetan Buddhism and its practice. It is important to know that "to understand precisely" may take some time. Through a step-by-step process of familiarization, application, inner introspection, and practice, our understanding will deepen. Little by little, our mind will naturally attune to the actual meaning of the Dharma as we walk this path of wisdom.

The Preparation

The path of wisdom begins with the taking of Refuge. Refuge means a safe haven where we are protected from the wrong[3] paths, the wrong ideas, and the wrong actions. From the moment we take Refuge until we become enlightened, we seek refuge in the Buddha, the Dharma, and the Sangha. Collectively, they are known as the Three Jewels, or the Triple Gem.

In the Buddha we establish a link to the special qualities that Buddha Shakyamuni had accomplished. The Dharma encompasses all of his teachings and methods to develop the enlightened qualities. We need someone to teach us the Dharma, someone who has successfully achieved the results by his own efforts. He is

---

[3] The term "wrong" in the context of Buddhism means "that which creates suffering," or "that which does not lead to enlightenment". It is synonymous with "harmful", "negative" or "non-virtuous." On the contrary, "right", "correct", "beneficial", "positive" and "virtuous" are terms which connote that which leads to enlightenment, or liberation from suffering.

someone who has learnt the teachings, and has put them into practice and achieved the results. He is thus a realized being. He may not have the complete realization of a Buddha. Nevertheless, he has achieved certain qualities that he can now transmit to others. He is an accomplished spiritual master and a qualified teacher. We can rely on him to impart his knowledge and skills to us. We, therefore, take refuge in him and others like him who are the "extraordinary Sangha."

The word, Sangha[4], means "the gathering of those endowed with virtuous aspirations". There are generally two kinds of Sangha: the ordinary and the extraordinary Sangha. Ordinary Sangha refers to any community of Buddhist teachers from whom we can obtain teachings. A gathering of Dharma practitioners can also be referred to as a Sangha. But it is the extraordinary Sangha as explained in whom we seek refuge.

We start with the basic meaning of Refuge as protection. As our knowledge and understanding increase with practice, we will come to appreciate a broader and deeper meaning of Refuge. But first, we have to prepare. What does it mean to prepare? To prepare means we begin by listening to the teachings. We can learn from the Buddhist teachers who can impart a lot of information and explanations about the Dharma. We can also learn by reading the written Dharma texts. This is what is meant by listening (*tö* in Tibetan) to the teachings. Having listened to the

---

[4] *Gendun* in Tibetan

teachings, we then reflect (*sam* in Tibetan) and integrate the teachings into our thinking so as to reach a deeper understanding of their meanings. This is how we prepare.

For what are we preparing? The goal of all Dharma teachings is to awaken our own mind and nothing more. When we have achieved this goal, we are said to be enlightened or have attained Buddhahood. These are just terms that may at times be confusing to us. Actually, enlightenment cannot be confined to terms and concepts. We talk about enlightenment, but for now, it is merely the projection of an idea. We are not really clear about its meaning. Enlightenment signifies a mind that is clear and stable, free from ignorance. It is a state of mind called *sangye* in Tibetan. *Sang* means completely clear, pure, and free of all stains. *Gye* means knowledge in the fullest extent, or all encompassing knowledge. Therefore, *sangye* is a mind free from ignorance, free from preconceived or fixed notions, yet it knows clearly and completely.

The enlightened mind is thus a clear mind without any ignorance or veils. The adjective "clear" is sometimes misunderstood. It does not mean clear as in light. To clear our mind of veils does not mean to reject all the good things either. There is no need to reject the positive feelings, the nice appearances, etc. They are a part of normal living, a good way of living, but they are not our main goal in life. Clarity of mind will appear by itself. We can't get it from somewhere and nobody can give it to us.

Ultimately, everything will clear by itself. This is what *sangye* means. Any attempt to explain it is limited by words. Therefore, the deeper meaning of *sangye* has to be understood or experienced by oneself.

Our mind can become more open and clearer if we engage in a correct practice regularly. Any opening in mind actually lends itself to further opening. But while the mind is not too clear, it will take time before any result becomes apparent. For example, some people who are very knowledgeable or educated find that the more they know, the more they don't know. When we don't believe that there is more to learn we stop searching. After all, it is our wish to know our true nature that has led us to the Dharma. The more we understand our own mind, the clearer we will become. Once we have reached a certain level, then the many detailed explanations are no longer necessary. But until we do, we analyze and question the details in order to understand more precisely. When we see the real meaning, or when we know, then everything is clear.

As explained already, the ultimate goal for any Buddhist is to reach a state of perfect clarity or Buddhahood. It is important to focus on this goal. We try to be clear, to be properly directed towards our goal. It means to practice the teachings because they help us get clearer. The opposite of clarity is confusion which is connected to ignorance[5].

---

[5] The Tibetan term is *marikpa*, or *avidya* in Sanskrit. In the Buddhist context, this word does not refer to an intellectual deficiency but to a fundamental error in interpretation.

One example of ignorance is thinking that we understand when we don't. Ignorance does not mean stupid. It means that there is no clear understanding of how things are. Ignorance is like not being able to see beyond a wall because our view is blocked. When the mind is clear, there is nothing to block our view. In *sangye*, there is no blockage, no ignorance and no mental veils. Mind is clear and it sees limitlessly. This is very difficult for us to fathom because we are limited by our physical body, and by our physical world. But the true nature of mind is completely clear. We have to constantly remind ourselves of this clarity aspect of mind because we have to become very familiar with it. Otherwise, in the next moment, clarity is forgotten and we are thrown back in our usual ways.

How we relate and apply the teachings in our own lives is very important. People who are new to the Dharma may find it difficult to understand because they may not be seeking enlightenment at all. Then, there are people who are not sure what it is they are looking for. They may wish to better understand about life, for instance. But whatever it is that people desire, they will also need the Dharma. It is like buying a house. We may not be concerned about having a garden at the time of looking, but once we have comfortably settled in a house, we will begin to think about adding a nice garden, etc. It is the same when we first relate to the Dharma. Our focus may be to solve our problems at first, or how to become more productive in life. We generally pick the parts of the teachings that suit us and apply them to our own situations. Regardless of our original impetus in seeking out the Dharma, we will no doubt continue to feel that we are missing something, and so we continue to look deeper. This is why it is important to have an open mind and try not to restrict our vision.

It is not good to rely on the teachings when we have a problem only and to forget about it when the problem passes. By doing more and more practice, by listening more and more to the teachings, we will very slowly begin to open ourselves. Gradually, we will become clearer about ourselves. Our understanding will increase which will in turn benefit others as well. It will also strengthen our resolve that enlightenment is indeed very important to us. In our daily life, we will find that our actions become increasingly congruous with the Dharma. But in the beginning, most people don't have this wish for enlightenment. Therefore, the teachers who understand the inclination of the different people try to include key points that are useful to them both for the short-term, as well as for the long-term.

Up until now, we are used to our own thinking. We think about ourselves and our own benefit. This comes easy and natural to all of us. But when we are asked to broaden our scope, we find that our mind is very limited. Our attitudes and ideas are somewhat narrow and biased. When we want something, we push to achieve the result. We are constantly moving forward, pushing to achieve results, one after another. We have been like this all along. But to achieve enlightenment, or to achieve a clear mind is quite different. It is not a fixed result that we can obtain. The path to enlightenment encompasses extensive knowledge and many qualities. Each of us must seek to gradually develop our understanding and clarity of mind.

Needless to say, everything depends on our own efforts. After we listen to the teachings with an open mind, we take the time to reflect on the meaning. Through introspection, we will begin to understand. We will have a slightly different expectation in our practice as well as in our daily lives. This expectation does not block us. In fact, it directs us further into a deeper understanding and more clarity. We are then able to experience differently as we live and practice. The change can come about only if we take the time to integrate the teachings in our lives and practice. Always remember the process of listening, reflecting, and integrating. It is a continuous and gradual process which prepares us for the ultimate goal of enlightenment.

Understanding
the Way We Function

Yeshe is a Tibetan term which signifies wisdom that is non-fabricated, without discrimination and judgment. It is seeing clearly without any blockage or limits. To live in the Dharma means to live without grasping or rejecting. We can only function based on our current capacity but we can make an effort to live differently connected to *yeshe*.

When we examine our own situations in the normal functions of everyday life, we have many questions. By applying the Dharma, the questions will clear up. In other words, we join together the two parts. The first part is the Dharma teachings and explanations which show us how things are, and how we are. The second part is our present conditions – what is happening in our lives now. We want to combine these two parts. We analyze each condition, difficulty, or situation in our own lives and determine whether what the Dharma tells us is true or not. Do the conditions and ideas as presented by the Dharma apply to us? Do the meanings as explained by the Dharma apply in our particular set of circumstances? By examining in this way, we are essentially relating the meaning of the Dharma to our own lives. As a result, we will become clearer about the meaning of the teachings and about ourselves. It is always when we are looking for a solution to a problem that we have a chance to get clearer. And when we are presented with an explanation of something, if we just try to understand it immediately, it is not all that clear. We have to take the time to check and analyze the meanings properly before we can arrive at a real understanding.

THE OBSCURATIONS

It is important to know that our perception is tainted by karma in the mind which has its roots in ignorance. Because of karma, our understanding and knowledge are obscured or tainted. How does karma taint our mind? The results of karma give rise to obscuration that reside in mind. An obscuration acts as a veil, which covers, distorts, and taints our perception. As a result, we do not recognize the true nature of things and of ourselves. In general we speak of three classifications of obscuration which are the causes of suffering for sentient beings (*semchen* in Tibetan):

- obscuration caused by habitual tendencies;
- obscuration caused by conceptual knowledge, or

obscuration caused by preconceived and fixed notions;

• obscuration caused by *nyönmong*[6] or disturbing emotions.

The nature of mind is obscured by the habitual tendencies. It is easier for us to see the causes of our habits in our current life. One example is our upbringing which includes many values and customs acquired during our formative years that are now ingrained in us as habits. In the teachings, it is explained that habits are formed in previous lives as well.

We all function in similar ways, for example, when we think we know something, we believe it and we are convinced of it. At the same time, we are blocked by it. When we then encounter something contrary to what we already know, we cannot accept it right away and want to reject it. In other words, our mind is blocked by what we already know. This is actually normal. It is human nature, not only human nature, but the nature of living beings who live an illusory and conditioned existence yet believing in it as real[7]. We cannot say the way we are is right or wrong because our capacity is blocked. If we are set in what we are used to, then when faced with

---

[6] *Nyönmong* in Tibetan, or *klesha* in Sanskrit, points to any mental factor that produces an obscuring effect on the mind. Disturbing emotions such as anger, jealousy, desire, pride, etc is one translation of this term. Other translations are: emotions, passions, afflictions.

[7] *The* "illusory and conditioned existence" of living beings is commonly known as *samsara*.

something different, our tendency will be to reject it. Likewise, when we know something, we no longer question or judge it. We accept it as real rather than illusory. However, if we can understand that every condition is neither right nor wrong, but it is important to work with it, then there is more room for us to maneuver, to adapt, or to change our position. In that sense, we actually gain more freedom – a liberation of mind. We try to understand the different aspects of our conditions without grasping or getting stuck in them. Neither do we reject them. This is the vantage point for all our activities in daily life which will enable us to understand others as well, which is our main goal at the relative[8] level.

The point is to be natural. There is nothing extraordinary in reflecting on the teachings, and in relating to them in our daily lives yet it is important to do so. Dharma should be part of our everyday functioning if we want results. It is not special so we stay relaxed and natural. We can apply the meaning of the Dharma to any circumstance as it happens during the course of our day. Therefore every situation is useful to us. We use it to become clearer about the exact meaning of each essential point of Dharma. Gradually, we will come to a deeper understanding.

When we see something directly by ourselves, the understanding stays in the mind and

---

[8] *Relative* here pertains to our current association or experience of the phenomenal world as opposed to an enlightened mind's *ultimate* or *absolute* experience of the true nature of mind and of phenomena.

works for us. The problem is we never get the meaning exactly. It is because we are always influenced by our veiled perceptions so we need to be aware of our tendencies. Our habits are always with us, and they influence how we think leading on to how we feel and act. The concepts which we have adopted through living in the world and through socialization also have the same hold on us. Even our emotions, how we feel and react so automatically at times are our tendencies. We have never paid attention to our tendencies. We think we are just the way we are, and so we never get the proper view. We feel that what we are used to is normal and yet we sense our lives superficial. The point is not to think life superficial or that it is not right. Try to think more precisely when faced with actual situations rather than following the usual tendencies. Apply the Dharma and examine more carefully. Gradually, we will get a clearer understanding of how things are, which will enable us to relate to them without the influence of our tendencies.

Take for example a walk in the field where you see many plants and flowers in different colors, and shapes. Observe how you feel and your internal dialogue. You may find thoughts like, *"This is good, this is not good, this is nice, this is not nice."* When you are not aware, your thinking just goes on like that. It is normal. The little judgments occupy the mind. They come from our tendencies and concepts which we have adopted. The concepts may have come from other people's opinions. You heard them and have adopted them as your own so you also think, *"Oh yes, this is good."* Concepts are also based on what is widely considered as acceptable versus what is not. You should try to see more into such conventions and values. What is good or bad really comes from what you have been used to as you live and conform in society. For example, someone tells you that dandelions are common weeds whereas orchids are rare and exquisite flowers. When you hear enough of it, you will start to think that way, too. However, on your own without outside influence, try to get a fresh perspective, you will actually see differently.

Much of our thinking is based on our tendencies. Whether our mind is happy or not depends on how we interpret the circumstances. It is important to get free of our tendencies. Where there is no grasping, nothing is there. We just go for a walk in the field, and look around. If we are fresh in the moment, we can see very clearly. We are aware of our opinions and discriminations which don't matter so much. What matters is to see clearly, to see things as they are which is what mind is capable of doing. Therefore we choose to work with each situation as it is because we can.

Our life is very similar to a walk in the field. There are many things and many complications. But if we really look, it is not so complicated, difficult, or heavy. Rather, it is the load of our habits, opinions, and thinking that we bring to every situation that makes it complicated and heavy. We feel overwhelmed at times. But look more deeply, and you will find that there is really nothing. If you lean too much in one way, or if you specialize too much in certain subjects, you can actually become off-balance. This is why the advice is to use our skill sets but still maintain a little distance or space and a broader perspective. This makes the mind more open. Even the seemingly important conditions are actually not so difficult to deal with. We remain "fresh". A fresh thought and wisdom is there so everything is very easy to understand in all its conditions. This is an alternative way. If we can steer clear of the obscurations caused by our conceptual knowledge, our habitual tendencies, and our disturbing emotions, regardless of whether they are good or bad, our mind will become clear then we can work with anything.

As explained already, we are in the middle between the way of the Buddha-dharma and the worldly way we are so accustomed to. Usually, we think the teachings are perfect and our life is not so easy or perfect. We want to be perfect but we cannot do it. We try perhaps to be as perfect as we can for a few hours but we cannot keep it up for the rest of the time. This is how we generally are. Actually, we can. We apply the teachings as much as we can by reflecting in this way, *"What do the teachings really mean? What do I have to do in my life-situation?"* then we can really make a connection. This is how we can become clearer, not just by remembering the words but to integrate the Dharma into how we are. The understanding will come easier to us and we will cope better with the circumstances.

THE EMOTIONS

The emotions are conditions of our mind. We should neither suppress nor develop them but understand them. When we do, everything becomes simpler to manage, our relationship with other people will become easier, and our connection to the Dharma the stronger. The converse is also true. When we don't understand our emotions, then everything becomes complicated. We are critical of others and ourselves. The emphasis again goes back to our own mind. All the teachings converge on this point. When we truly understand the conditions of our mind, we will see things as they are. To us, a toothache is real and not an illusion. But when we see the real nature of mind, we will experience the pain as illusory. It is easy to talk about emotions. They feel very heavy to us because we have piled on them all kinds of concepts. We are ever trying to keep the good feelings and steer clear of the bad ones. This is normal and there is nothing wrong with it. But, the negative emotions cannot be driven away because they are not different from mind, they are mind.

The question is: what can we do? Everybody has experienced counterproductive emotions: anger, jealousy, unhappiness, pride, and many others. We think that if only we could get rid of them, we would be happy. This is wrong. We need to look at the cause of these negative emotions, the cause of anger, the cause of jealousy, the cause of attachment, the cause of pride, and the cause of expectation. Since the emotions are our mind, the only solution is to realize the true nature of mind. We will then see how the negative emotions don't make sense and they will dissolve on their own. The process of realizing the nature of mind is of course not easy, and it takes a long time. However, we should not be discouraged. The teachings advise us to always be aware of a situation and its related conditions. We practice looking at mind and its orientation. We see that we have desires and expectations. When they are not satisfied, our negative emotions come up. This is always the case. It is very important that we understand this basic functioning in ourselves as well as in others. Simply look without trying to get rid of anything. This is how we work with the emotions in the beginning.

An agitated mind or a mind without peace gives rise to emotions. We are so habituated to our emotional process that it is difficult to keep it separate. As a result, we cannot see an emotion for what it is. Whenever our mind is in some kind of discomfort such as anger, sadness, or a mild depression, it is fodder for practice. In other words, we use the distressed mind to verify the teachings. In this way, we have a chance to experience the actual meaning of the teachings spontaneously in our mind, beyond what words or a mere conceptual understanding can afford us. In the beginning, the weaker emotions may prove easier for this purpose. For example, when we are a little unhappy, we try to see how mind is linked to the emotion. What is the cause of the unhappiness? Is it pride, attachment, ignorance, or hatred? Try to be honest and clear about the cause because by habit, we reach for excuses. It is easy to say, *"I'm unhappy because of this or that."* But if we are truthful and really get at the source of our discontent, we will gain some insight, which we call *denpa* in Tibetan.

Denpa means the truth without any excuse or compromise. *Denpa* points to the real situation of mind. Our mind tends to sidetrack from the truth, making it tricky to walk straight into a situation and meeting it head on. Simply look at a situation without adding any feelings to it. Our tendency is to look for something important. *"I need this, or I have to do that."* We are always aiming for something. To look unconditionally without purpose is foreign to us. We have to learn how to do it. As we look, we avoid trying to get rid of something or to achieve a better result. We have neither the desire to gain anything nor expectations.

Take for example, you are walking and you fall. Look at the cause of your fall. Is it because of your shoes, the road, or the way you walk? Look without any attitude or preconceived ideas. Just look naturally. Similarly we look at the distractions of mind. The point is not to try to solve the problem but to see the mental conditions that generated the problem in the first place. This will give us a clear answer which will come on its own. It is actually quite difficult to do. But if we keep trying to look as described, eventually, everything will become clearer to us. Very slowly, we will gain *ngepa*, which means certainty – a very clear understanding which enables us to work on ourselves. This may sound simple but to actually try to do it can be confusing because of our emotional states and conditions. Nevertheless, we have to learn to work with them so we practice and try to follow the instructions.

The Dharma elucidates the real nature of mind and of all phenomena. We may have an intellectual understanding of it. *Denpa* or "truth" points to the truth of mind, the truth of all conditions. We need to see and realize it for ourselves. In other words, we have to experience *denpa*. We try to see the nature of mind and the nature of our emotions without doubt or hesitation. We do it not because somebody told us to do so but we just try to see the truth.

Take the example of our situation here in *samsara*. There is happiness and there is sadness. While we continue to seek happiness in our usual ways, we can also take the time to do the practice, to try to have a clear and peaceful mind. Clarity of mind can produce two positive effects for us. One is our total involvement in the task at hand, and the other is having a clear view of what we are doing. So the point is to watch ourselves. We watch ourselves while we practice, while we work, during difficult times, during times of enjoyment, all the time. In this way, we try to keep separate our awareness from the normal functions in life. "Separate" in this context means to be able to look at ourselves in any given moment be it of great joy or sadness like watching a movie. When we can do it, even if we feel very sad, somehow we understand that it is all right. This may sound a bit strange yet it is a very important point. You should try and see for yourself. If it is too difficult for you to understand it now then keep it as useful information for the future.

Whenever we feel at a loss to see the nature of something, we refer to the teachings for clarification and guidance. In everyday life, when we are confused about something, we can find an explanation for it. But with respect to our emotion, we want to see it for what it is. For example, we generally think of ourselves as very important which happens to be why individually we are in our life situations. Let's say you have broken your arm and it is very painful. If you look, you will see that you identify with your arm. It is you. Even if you tell yourself the pain is illusory you cannot leave it alone. You have to attend to the soreness. Another way is to see your arm as separate from your mind, then the pain in the arm is also separate and it makes it easier to cope. You know you broke your arm, the cause and the resulting conditions. The point of this kind of analysis is to separate the mind from the arm which can make the mind clearer. As a result, you will experience the pain differently and you will also understand your mind differently. Without this kind of check in place, your mind and the pain are stuck together. Then there is a lot of suffering and confusion. These are then two ways of looking at the incident of a broken arm.

We can apply these two ways to examine external events that we encounter as well as our inner feelings or emotions. First try to see how we identify with them because otherwise, they cannot have contact with our mind. By maintaining some distance from our thoughts and actions, we can be more in tune with our mind and its movements. "Not identifying" with thoughts and actions, etc. does not mean we are nonchalant or we don't care as in thinking, *"Nothing matters."* As long as we are here in *samsara*, we are careful in everything we do. The point is to also keep a watchful eye on how we are engaged in daily situations, in our emotional states and their causes. By watching and being aware in this way, we will gain further understanding and clarity.

By habit, we are discriminating given any situation but we ought to see accurately or know what is of value. For example, there is nothing wrong in being actively involved and not wasting time. Without question, we are connected to our individual habits, background and culture, they are the relative conditions in our mind. There is nothing to add or reject. We accept whatever situation, or state of mind we are in, keep a little detached, and be aware. This is already a preparation to meditation.

Meditation means to be aware and not to be distracted by thoughts. For now, it is very difficult not to be distracted in our daily life. Our thoughts are very strong at the moment. However, we should still try to be aware whenever we can. We should try to see a little differently than what we are used to. Often we find that we don't have time to be aware, or to see things differently, or we just don't know how. We may not be interested or motivated enough to do so. We may feel overwhelmed by too much information and cannot decide on a best method for us. But it is really not all that confusing even though it is understandable that we find it so.

Actually, we can apply the watchful state in all situations without pressure during practice, lectures, and daily life. And we should not force ourselves either. Simply be aware without any preconceived notions because we will be able to see clearer. If we can't do it constantly, we can try from time to time. The more we do, the easier it will be. We need to understand that this watchful state is important because it prepares us for meditative practices. In short, we need to practice this way of seeing clearly to really experience it for ourselves.

The Four Thoughts

In general, any meditative practice begins with what is called "the preliminary practices". They support and prepare practitioners for more advance meditation. The "Contemplation on the Four Thoughts" is an indispensable preliminary practice because it directly influences the choices we make in our lives. Very briefly, the Four Thoughts are:

• To contemplate the precious human existence;
• To contemplate impermanence;
• To contemplate karma;
• To contemplate the result of karma - suffering.

At first glance, these concepts seem simple and straightforward enough. But perhaps due to a lapse in understanding, doubt creeps in and we find excuses to downplay their significance. Or when we feel unable to deal with the "Four Thoughts," we choose to block them out. This is normal. Unconsciously, we avoid the difficult things preferring to cover them up with something nice and just look at the cover, like hiding the unfinished wood of a shrine with a nice fabric. It is the same in our life situation, when we don't want to see precisely, we turn away or make up some nice commentary about it. But if your arm is broken, talking nicely around it or covering it up with fabric won't help. You need to treat it. On the other hand, facing life's real situation does not mean we have to be pessimistic and suffer either. The key is to reflect properly on the Four Thoughts to understand the truths in their meanings.

TO CONTEMPLATE THE PRECIOUS HUMAN EXISTENCE

The first of Four Thoughts is "to contemplate the precious human existence." Immediately, there is a tendency to think of the overpopulation in China or India and human life does not seem all that valuable or precious anymore! Somehow, we have overlooked ourselves. The precious human life means exactly that our very life is precious. We should try to make good choices, and live our lives in a meaningful way. If you are doing something wrong, you should stop. You should also protect yourself from harm. For instance, you have to fly somewhere but something is wrong with the plane, so you find an alternative way. Sometimes an attitude such as, *"I don't care,"* may set in and you ignore the risks. Sometimes, with one stroke of the brush, you paint everything as being *"OK"* when it is not. These attitudes are what we call illusions. Don't get caught up in them. Try to be honest with yourself and do what is best or what is necessary in your life. The precious human being is you and your own potential. It means to constructively use your very good opportunity here. This is the point.

The Buddha Shakyamuni said that all beings, not only humans, have the potential of becoming a Buddha. But it is in a human body that we can achieve the realization of a Buddha. Our profound nature, this potential for Buddhahood, is entirely free from the confusions of the samsaric mind. Realization of Buddhahood means in part to be free from confusion. We have this chance now so we should not waste it. Our worldly focus is always in trying to obtain things, things that are temporary and superficial. There is hardly any time for proper reflection. We should try to think in a broader scope and for the long term. It makes sense to invest our efforts to achieve benefits that will last because mind never ends, it will not dissolve. At the same time, we want to be free from suffering, free from ignorance. This life is important because we can act in a beneficial way now to really make a difference for our future.

According to the law of "actions and results" (to be explained later) the fact that we are here as humans is a result of our past deeds or actions. If we continue to act meaningfully then we will again be reborn in good conditions. Good conditions are conditions that afford us the freedom to engage in Dharma practice: like being born in a time and place where authentic teachers teach the Buddha-dharma; or not born with a handicap that would prevent us from understanding and practicing the Dharma teachings. We also don't want to find ourselves lacking in the capacity to believe in anything because then there will be nothing worthwhile to do. We want to have compassion and the capacity to develop it. Liberation from *samsara* does not mean to abandon the world. Actually, it means freedom from suffering whereby one works for the benefit of others.

All these conditions are described in detail by Gampopa in *The Jewel Ornament of Liberation* as good conditions encompassed in the meaning of a precious human birth. Everybody has Buddha-nature but the absence of any of these positive conditions would make it difficult to pursue the Dharma. Sometimes even when we know what is beneficial for us and we want to develop our mind, we are still held back by our desires, attachments, and habits. For example, you are offered a very good job in a very nice area with a nice apartment. But you turn it down preferring to stay with your existing job where there is a lot of pressure and the living conditions are quite harsh. You think to yourself that you cannot leave because you cannot let go of what you are used to. Because of your attachments, you are unable to change to a better situation. We have to let go of this type of attachment. Otherwise, we are blocking ourselves.

It is wrong to only acknowledge that yes, human life is precious, and then forget it. We already know the many conditions necessary to make the human life precious. To be reborn again in the next life with the same good conditions requires us to develop a way of thinking and acting now that can increase our understanding of mind as much as possible. This is the way to procure a better future.

You may have heard that the Dharma methods can bring about enlightenment in one lifetime. That is true, but for that to happen, one needs to learn, understand and genuinely apply the teachings. In any case, this is not the most important point for us. Rather, it is that each of us has the capacity to do this. A reincarnated teacher or practitioner is not particularly special. He happens to be someone who is practicing successfully and is therefore able to continue the same path in the next life. To continue means not to lose the capacity already achieved.

In general, we take for granted our human existence. Many things seem important to us yet we neglect to recognize what is really beneficial to us in the long run. When our time has run out, it is too late. So the First Thought aims not to pressure us but to motivate us to make the right choices in life. It prepares us by giving the reasons why Dharma practice is indispensable. We can see for ourselves the transitory nature of life's conditions for every living being. We can look to the Buddhist masters from the past as our role models and follow in their footsteps. For instance, they took their own future seriously.

They recognized the value in practicing the Dharma progressing life after life until enlightenment. If we use our good conditions and steer our practice in the same direction, then we too will achieve the same result.

Expectations are usually either for the short or long term. A practitioner who already recognizes the transitory nature of life's conditions can work directly for long-term goals. But most people lose sight of long-term goals, which are too difficult to fathom. They need to try harder and think deeper in order to look beyond the here and now.

People are more concerned with solving immediate problems and achieving short-term goals. Their problems are often related to the emotions and relationships, which are never-ending. One problem solved is always followed by another one. There are others who think that by avoiding people and the emotions then they can have peace. But they are just trying to escape rather than solving the problem. In fact, there is nothing to reject. We simply watch ourselves. See if we can make a connection to the meaning of the precious human life. From time to time, we do this. We do it in a very natural and spontaneous way. Very gradually, we will become clearer. Unless we really reflect and apply the meaning to ourselves, the truth of the precious human life is useless to us.

TO CONTEMPLATE IMPERMANENCE

The second of Four Thoughts emphasizes a conscious consideration of the impermanence of life and of all things. Once we have decided that Dharma practice is really worthwhile, we cannot put it off any longer. Time does not stop for anyone. Our actions and their corresponding results continue endlessly. We must try to increase clarity of mind while we are here. In a way, impermanence also means continuity because nothing stays the same. Everything continues to change and evolve.

An early chapter of the book, *"The Jewel Ornament of Liberation,"* explains the term, *samsara* and all its conditions. *Samsara* means cyclic existence. It is existence enmeshed within endless cycles of birth, sickness, aging, and death. The existence can consist of happiness and/or suffering. Each cycle ends at death when soon after another life begins – and so the cycles continue endlessly. There is no beginning either. Because we abhor suffering, we want to be free of it. But it will never happen unless we work on a proper solution or practice. The book then continues with Gampopa's teachings on the methods of liberation. We understand the conditions of suffering and that there is a way out. Because of impermanence, it follows then that liberation from suffering should be our main objective. We must stop wasting time.

It is not difficult to see the suffering of *samsara*. There are solutions and remedies to help us cope with the various life situations. But death, which is life's impermanence, seems to be the most challenging one of all. The contemplation on impermanence shows us how to cope with it. We prepare ourselves through achieving clarity of mind.

In life, we are used to the ups and downs. We find things difficult to bear at times while they seem not so intolerable at others. We want a comfortable life with good food and nice clothes. We are willing to work towards this goal knowing that there will be some roadblocks along the way but they won't stop us. We are not afraid instead we find ways to cope with the obstacles. It is the same with our goal to be liberated from suffering. And the point is then not to settle for temporary solutions but to evolve toward a definitive outcome.

The precious human life can bring us benefits beyond the present life. Ideally, we would like to be reborn continuously as humans practicing the Dharma until enlightenment. But life never stays unchanged not even for one moment. Mind's activities move in a constant flux. Impermanence means that time - each hour, minute, or instant is passing. The continuum of change is also subject to the law of cause and effect. We have to recognize that this is happening not to stress us out but so that we can integrate this insight into our normal functioning.

Through our life experiences, we begin to appreciate the meaning of the teachings. When we do, we strive to improve a little bit at a time by following the Dharma practice. This process cannot be emphasized enough because sometimes we don't want to listen and so we don't really hear properly. In the very least, we should be careful to avoid those actions that will bring us rebirth in bad conditions replete with great suffering.

The transition from the present life to the next life is a natural and automatic process. After we die, and before we take the next rebirth, there is an in-between period called the *bardo*. The mind experiences then its most powerful tendencies, without the body being there to alleviate them. Next, the mind will take rebirth so there will again be birth, growth, and dying. Our achievement in practice during our lifetime will also help us in the *bardo*. When we have practiced a lot, we will realize that liberation from the cycle of existence is the only way out.

Liberation means freedom from the present condition of not being able to see clearly. Liberation delivers a clear mind that can go through all the different conditions in life as well as in the *bardo*. This clarity is really not so difficult to achieve if we follow the methods and put in the effort. Granted, we need to have the proper conditions but the good news is that all Dharma practices give us all these favorable conditions.

We have to go beyond the common meaning of impermanence. It is not enough to just acknowledge it. We need to reflect carefully on its meaning, on its significance in our lives and its impact on our choices. We scrutinize how impermanence affects our day-to-day experience. We want to be markedly aware of impermanence without fear, surprise or excuses. We accept it as a normal part of our lives.

Everyday, we drink coffee. There is no element of surprise about it, just part of every day life. In the same way, impermanence is a part of every day life. Students studying in school usually take for granted the material that they already know. They focus and spend time studying and remembering the ideas and information unfamiliar to them. But with impermanence, it is a little different. Though we already know it, we don't take it for granted. Impermanence is a bit heavy to deal with, nevertheless, we start by seeing it a little at a time. It will soon give meaning to what we do, then it will be very useful. So we accustom ourselves to seeing impermanence. We don't have to be stressed over it but try to slowly get used to this view so it becomes a positive habitual tendency of mind. Like the clothes we wear every day, we know our wardrobe so we can decide accordingly. We wash our clothes when they get dirty. We take more care with our nicer clothes by not sitting in dirty places for instance. How we wear and care for our clothes is very simple and straightforward, nothing complicated. And so it is the same with the habit of seeing impermanence. It is awareness without ignorance, in full view of the meaning of impermanence.

TO CONTEMPLATE KARMA

In Tibetan, three words together form the translation of the term "karma": *le gyu dre* meaning action, cause and effect. In general, "karma" and "causes and effects" are used interchangeably. The third of Four Thoughts is the contemplation of karma. Our understanding of karma can influence us towards acting in a more beneficial way.

We can say that in general, situations and circumstances we encounter are the results of causes we have created in the past. More often than not, we see ourselves as victims of what is happening. We always wonder why certain events happen to us. The basic premise of karma is: every thought produces a result whether or not it is acted out. We don't realize that our negative thoughts yield negative effects. Karma comes from our mind, our speech, and our actions. A mistaken notion is that only our actions cause the results. But if we did not have the thought in the first place, then no speech or action would follow. Sometimes we act and nothing comes of it, while at other times, our action makes a difference. In both instances, karma is created regardless of whether our action comes to fruition or not. Moreover, the teachings explain that whether the karma is neutral, positive, or negative, corresponds directly to our original intention, be it neutral, positive, or negative. This is in fact the natural and infallible law of karma – the truth of karma, a reason compelling enough to make us pay attention to our thoughts, and motivation.

When we understand the process of causes and results, we will know how to be careful so as to avoid the negative actions. Even when negative thoughts arise in our mind, we can choose not to cower under their influence. For example, in the moment when we want to take revenge on someone to return the harm done to us, if we can recognize that it will only generate more causes and effects which can backfire at us at some point, we will not do it. We can choose instead to resolve the conflict by a calm discussion without harming the other. Sometimes we feel as if we are forced to act in a negative way, but with the understanding of karma in mind, we know it is worth our while to choose to react in a positive way. It is certainly possible for us to override the thoughts, emotions and negative feelings that arise in the mind without following them. Therefore, the understanding of karma help us pick the right course of action so we can lead our lives in the best possible direction. On the contrary, if we always react on impulse, then we would only create more negative conditions for our life now and in the future.

In particular, *samsara* or our existence is actually the result of karma. The results of karma are sometimes referred to as the defects of *samsara*. Understanding the impact of karma will naturally make us more careful in our intentions. We cannot avoid karma. In fact the more we try to avoid a situation, the more we become involved in it, and the more negative it will become for us. The way to deal with karma is somewhat similar to an earlier example of how we deal with our clothes – we are not worried yet we are aware and careful.

There is a relative dimension[9] to meditative practices that develops our inner qualities and

---

[9] The absolute aspect of meditative practices directly affects our progress on the Dharma path to enlightenment.

conditions which will in turn enhance beneficial action or karma. This increase in positive karma can produce favorable effects for an individual in family situations, in relationships, etc. There can also be good collective or group karma which comes from doing group meditation, for instance. The increase of positive potential also means the lessening of the negative. We should therefore choose not to harm others, to help those in need, in other words, do all we can to avoid creating negative conditions.

To Contemplate the Result of Karma - Suffering

The result of karma is not a judgment or sentence. Rather, the result happens naturally and spontaneously. Our thinking is conceptual. Our thoughts and ideas are general and abstract concepts which are inferred or derived from specific instances in our experience. They are therefore a construct of mind. Karma is different. We have to use a term to describe karma, so we use the term "law" even though there is no one there judging us. However, karma is like a law of nature. For instance, in nature, water is an essential condition for a flower to grow. Without water, the flower will dry up. It is the same with karma. Every karma created will produce a result, condition, or effect. When the effects gather together, ripen or mature, there will be an outcome.

It is due to karma that our mind is veiled or tainted by the three types of obscurations[10]. When we look carefully at our inner thinking, we will see that it is connected to our concepts, habits and emotions. How karma works is the same for positive and negative karma. For example, not wanting to harm others is one karma and wanting to harm others is another karma. Both are karmas that will give an effect whether or not we act on it. If we act on it, the result will be stronger.

The Buddha's first teaching was on suffering. The truth of suffering is also the first of his Four Truths of the Noble Ones[11]. The Buddha taught that by attaining enlightenment we can go beyond suffering. Right now, our conditions are unsatisfactory. The fact that we are alive means that we have to face suffering. Suffering comes from a fundamental clinging - a mind that clings to a self as truly existent or ego-clinging, which is *daktu dzinpa* in Tibetan. Ego-clinging creates a constant but very subtle form of suffering which we will call here, "fundamental suffering." The problem is we don't often feel this suffering. We can readily feel gross sufferings such as physical pain, but not this fundamental type of suffering.

Our existence in *samsara* is characterized by clinging to a self. In various spiritual traditions, suffering is a requisite to accomplish a practice. However, in the Buddha's teaching, it is ex-

---

[10] See chapter 2 for explanations.

[11] The Four Truths of the Noble Ones are: the truth of suffering, of the origin of suffering, of its cessation and of the path.

plained that we don't need to suffer (in the ordinary sense of the word) in order to reach enlightenment or any spiritual realization. Even though we don't have to suffer, we still need to understand suffering.

The Buddha taught that the type of suffering varies according to the different realms of existence in *samsara*. The drawings in the "wheel of existences"[12] depict the suffering generally experienced by the living beings in each of the six realms. For example, humans and animals experience suffering differently. As humans, our feelings and perception are different than those of the animals so we experience things differently. Animals are very close to us so it is possible for us to relate to some of their suffering but still we cannot experience what they experience. The same may be said of the other realms.

The human existence is characterized by strong desire entwined with other emotions. These obscurations of mind produce suffering causing us to react negatively thereby producing ever more negative causes. The mechanism of karma is subtle and complex. An action based on a very simple concept may produce a great variety of conditions making possible a correspondingly great variety of results. This is why we experience so many different types of suffering in the human realm. The Dharma teachings broadly classify the types of actions or causes

---

[12] It is a pictorial representation of *samsara* showing the six realms of conditioned existence of the: gods, angry gods, humans, animals, hungry ghosts, and hells.

along with their corresponding types of imprints in mind and resultant types of suffering.

The Dharma also explains that because of fundamental ignorance, desire and attachment are particularly strong in humans. As we know, every human follows his own ideas and opinions, right or wrong. When an opinion leads to an outright deed that is negative, it will result in suffering. Despite our efforts to act sincerely, due to the ignorance in mind, we make mistakes. Even when the mistake is not intentional, it will inevitably lead to suffering.

The Buddha's advice is to develop love and compassion towards every sentient being equally – commonly referred to as the enlightened attitude. Having this quality of mind will on the one hand, reduce the stream of negative thoughts thus deterring the negative actions. On the other, it will develop that which is beneficial.

This is why the urgency for us to generate the enlightened attitude cannot be overemphasized. Developing *bodhicitta*[13] is possible if we open ourselves to the suffering of other sentient beings. We develop this state of mind to help beings, ourselves included, to go beyond suffering. This attitude is the opposite of ego-clinging, a

---

[13] *Bodhicitta* or the enlightened attitude is the wish to reach perfect Buddhahood for the benefit of all beings. It has two aspects: relative and ultimate. The ultimate aspect recognizes the emptiness nature of mind and phenomena. The relative aspect of enlightened attitude manifests in two ways: in aspiration and in action. The wish for the welfare of all beings without exception is aspiration and the altruistic application of the aspiration is action.

stepping away from self-centeredness towards all others.

Once we understand the causes and effects of suffering, we appreciate the importance of the Dharma path and make real efforts to practice.

CONCLUDING NOTES ON THE FOUR THOUGHTS

In sum, to prepare and build the foundation of Dharma practice, we need to be aware of our thoughts, speech, and action as often as we can. We are aware in our practice as well as in daily activities. Eventually we will reach our goal. To be aware means to be conscious. The Four Thoughts are also referred to as the preliminaries. "Preliminary" in this context does not mean "prerequisite." It does not mean that we have to finish one step before going on to the next step. Rather, it means that to understand the next step, the previous step is very important. By reflecting and remembering the Four Thoughts, we can connect our Dharma practice to the daily life situations. At the same time, we are properly directed in the right motivation. In this way, we protect ourselves from negative thoughts and deeds.

We are all busy with work and family but individually, each of us decides on the degree of commitment on the Dharma path. The aim of the Four Thoughts is to remind us to take good care of our lives and not fall into the influence of negative thoughts. When we can clearly understand the conditions of living beings we will develop love and compassion towards them.

The negative thoughts will still arise in mind but the recall of these Four Thoughts will prevent us from being trapped in them. They also act as a positive remedy to fundamental ignorance.

The application of love and compassion means to be helpful and supportive of others based on our individual capacities. We will find that sometimes we can help and sometimes we cannot. Sometimes our help is not wanted so there is no point in trying. Being helpful also requires training. In the beginning it is more like an exercise. When we witness the sufferings of others, even when we cannot help, we can make wishes for their situations to improve. We cannot save the world but our mind can be directed towards the lessening of suffering for all.

The Enlightened Attitude and Practice

Bodhicitta is an altruistic motivation in all that we think, speak, and do. We avoid thinking only of ourselves to the exclusion of others. We try to be genuinely concerned for the suffering of all living beings. We wish them happiness and freedom from suffering. *Bodhicitta* is not just an idea but it is very profound in and of itself.

We begin by being slightly more open to others. Having an open mind enables us to care for others. We start to think more for others, then to share more with others, and then to be more beneficial to others. This is a learnt process through progressive training and practice. When we can act with *bodhicitta*, it is an indication that our practice is improving, that we are improving. We will find it increasingly easier and more natural to share everything beneficial with everyone.

All Buddhist teachings emphasize this one essential point: to generate the enlightened attitude, to open our mind. It doesn't matter that our mind is not fully open now or we can't do everything for others. The key is to start with ourselves right here and now. We try to connect with our own inner capacity whatever its current level. We do what is within our reach as much as possible. This is important. If we can open ourselves a little, then there is a basic quality in us that will expand and improve. At present, due to our ignorance, we have pride, greed, and other negative emotions. Under their influence, we tend to only want to do the "big" things. When we then realize that we cannot, we start to lose confidence in ourselves. Therefore, it is important to understand that we are not required to be at a certain level already with regards to our helpfulness to others. Rather, we do as much as we can in keeping with our own capability. This is what it means to engender *bodhicitta.*

Now we look at the practice of mind-training or *lojong,* a *bodhicitta* practice. *Lojong* means to put in place a positive motivation and attitude in lieu of the obscurations of mind, which are our habits, concepts, and negative emotions. *Lojong* means that which runs contrary to what we are used to. This positive attitude is a condition that we hold in our mind until gradually, over time, it shows up spontaneously in our thoughts and actions.

Lojong can bring about two kinds of result, a decrease in negative thoughts and action, and more importantly, an opportunity for a better

rebirth in the next life. After death, in the inter-
mediate state (*bardo* in Tibetan), the mind of a
deceased usually is still very much connected to
his tendencies while he was alive. After death,
those tendencies are released spontaneously one
connecting to the next and so on. The experiences in the *bardo* and in a dream state are quite
similar. He has not greater control over them in
the *bardo* than in his dreams. However, whatever progress achieved in meditation while alive
could serve him well in the *bardo*. This is in fact
one of the many applications of realization in
meditation. When a person falls asleep, he loses
momentarily total consciousness just before
sleep. His mind is there but completely disconnected. Even if he tries to see the transition from
being awake to sleeping, he is lost in it. He
passes into sleep without awareness. After some
time, he starts to dream. Throughout his sleep,
he is physically alive. The not knowing state is
referred to as a lack of realization – an inability
to see for himself what is happening to him. If
on the other hand he can go through the process
without ignorance, he will see the process of
sleeping - how he progresses into the sleep, and
then into the dream state. To him, dreaming
will not be a surprise anymore. He will see it as
just another state of mind. If he has this ability
(as a result of his training in meditation), then
we say that he realizes by himself what is going
on.

A mind without any realization can still have

positive tendencies. *Lojong*[14] practice can bring about this favorable effect. It places the mind in a positive condition and attitude where one is concerned for the benefit of other sentient beings. This entails a more open mind not influenced by negative disturbing emotions thus rendering the mind more flexible and considerate of others.

We can all see the suffering around us. Even if we don't see it immediately in our surroundings with our own eyes, we know that there is suffering for many people in different parts of the world. We know also the sufferings of the animals. These are very evident. We begin by feeling concerned for the suffering of others. Gradually, our concern will grow into love and compassion. This means to link our consciousness with love and compassion towards other sentient beings. We practice mind-training precisely to develop this link. Our motivation should not be based on our fear, or aversion to suffering, or a desire to find a way out only for the self. We are motivated by our concern for all sentient beings. In the beginning, our care and concern may be just a thought. In time, when we can see more and more, it will grow into a habit of mind. We will then understand the exact meaning of *bodhicitta.*

Take for instance when you watch television. You see that there is a lot of suffering and you

_____

[14] See Shamar Rinpoche, *The Path to Awakening, A Commentary on Ja Chekawa Yeshé Dorjé's Seven Points of Mind Training*: New Delhi, Motilal Barnasidass, 2009.

feel some pity for the people involved. That pity is only a thought. However, you don't really feel strongly for their predicament. But if the suffering were right in front of you, you would feel much differently. You would feel it very strongly. Our consideration for the welfare of others begins first as an idea. Progressively, we attempt to become more precise until we know what it means to be genuinely caring towards others. We care without passing judgment. We know that for every sentient being, the basic cause of suffering is ignorance, and so the mind is veiled by the three obscurations. We know that when we act through the negative tendencies, we create the conditions of suffering for ourselves. We know that everyone without exception is helplessly subject to these conditions. We therefore feel concern for everyone equally as we do ourselves. This is a fundamental principle that we must see for ourselves before we embark on any mind-training practices. We should check to ensure that our motivation is sincere. Some people might have other reasons for practicing mind-training. For them, the practice becomes a technical mental exercise, and nothing more.

In general, we place great value and importance in the result of whatever we do. The methods and means of achieving the results we don't regard as important. For example, you want to make a table. You don't think much of the tools. Your main focus is the end result, which is the table. When the table is made, the tools are put away and they don't matter much anymore.

Dharma practice, however, is not like that. All the conditions that we encounter along the path are very important. The engendering of love and compassion is an important condition from beginning to end. We begin our daily practice by raising the feeling of concern for all sentient beings by praying for them. Our practice also ends with prayers or wishes. We pray for favorable conditions beneficial for all sentient beings.

When we recite prayers, we try to adapt our mind to the meaning of the recited words. It is customary to say prayers before every teaching. Individually, we pray to make wishes that will benefit ourselves and others, and to express what we wish to do. Praying also integrates our wishes within ourselves into a habit of mind. Praying is not for calming the mind. First, we pray and make wishes. Then we listen to the teachings. Then we practice and apply what we have learnt. Finally, we think, speak, and act in accordance to our wishes. This is the process. Our whole way of being is thus linked to our wishes in our prayers. This is why we always pray sincerely to be properly directed.

Here is a basic wishing prayer which many practitioners recite daily:

"May all sentient beings have happiness, and its cause.
May they be free from suffering, and its cause.
May they never be separated from the supreme bliss free of suffering.
May they come to rest in the great equanimity free of attachment and aversion to those near and far."

In the first two lines of the prayer, we wish all beings to have happiness and the cause of happiness. We wish them to be free from suffering and the cause of suffering. The "cause" comes from karma, action and result. This applies to everybody including the person who is praying. These wishes are on a relative level while we are living in the phenomenal world. Ultimately, we wish them to gain realization of the mind and thus be set free from *samsara*. This basic prayer should precede any practice in which we may engage. This is not just a technique but it is *lojong*. We must sincerely attempt to embrace in our hearts a benevolent attitude. Otherwise, the prayer and our practice are reduced to words again. We should also not feel obligated to say the prayer. We must sincerely reflect on our wish for all beings until it is a genuine, natural, and positively directed.

The third line of the prayer is our wish that all beings never to be separated from a state of authentic joy that is without suffering. This brings us to a mind in equanimity, which is the resultant state of a Buddha as stated in the fourth line. Equanimity is very difficult to comprehend and it can be misunderstood. It points to a state of mind that does not differentiate between the self and others. It is a mind that is very clear and absent of disturbances as in Buddha-mind. A mind that is inseparable from authentic joy is a mind not distracted, thus free from all attachments. A mind that is distracted has no peace. We wish everyone to achieve, to realize this authentic joy. The realization of the awakened mind is a realization of a state of mind that is free of suffering, which implies freedom from ignorance.

In theory, we can all agree that love and compassion are good qualities which are beneficial for us to develop. It may take a long time before we can see the actual results for ourselves. The same can be said of negative traits, the causes of negative emotions.

To understand our emotions, we begin by slowing down and really try to see the connections between our motivations, expectations, and emotions. Through the many different incidents in daily life, we can observe how our emotions function. We try to see the circumstances in which they arise and how they make us react. This will lead us to recognize how mind functions with and without the emotions. This same process can be applied to any distraction of mind. We try to be aware of the conditions associated with the distraction, how it comes about and the resultant effects on us. For example, we may notice that when our expectation is not met we become angry. We have to take the time to slow down and look then. Then one day, we will see the causes for our own afflictions. We will at the same time understand it is the same in others. Realizing this sameness, this equality in all living beings by our bondage to our conditions, we will come to understand the state of equanimity, which is the result of knowing the functioning of our own mind.

The Dharma tells us that all the emotions and disturbances of mind come from ego-clinging. Through Dharma practice, we try to get free of this clinging to a self. Yet in a way, we cannot really say "free", because the "self" does not really exist in the first place. There is no "I". However, theoretically, we can loosen our grip to a self when we understand how mind functions. When we are able to work with the negative emotions and tendencies, then it is liberation. Liberation means to loosen the clinging. It sounds easy, *"Loosen up"*. But it is not so easy when we actually try. We find the self-clinging very strong. Some fear is also involved because we are addicted to this clinging. It can be intimidating to let go of an addiction. This is why to be liberated, we have to understand the actual functioning of the disturbing states of mind, how they arise, and their effects on us. The discovery is a slow and gradual process.

We are so used to being a certain way, and we think we are normal and good. Actually, mind is just being directed by thoughts such as, *"I should do this,"* or *"I should not do that,"* or *"This is good and that is bad."* If we look deeper, we may see more. We need to reflect and try to see what really is the meaning behind what we do, why we are the way we are. We need to see our habitual tendencies, and attitudes, then we will know more clearly about ourselves.

Because we cannot force a result, we progress a little at a time, day by day. When faced with some difficulty, rather than wanting it to disappear, which is normal, we try to look at the experience. When we hear on the news that someone has been attacked, we may feel a little alarmed but then we carry on as usual. We are so desensitized to bad news that we regard them as mere daily events. We have become apathetic. The point is even when we don't really care, we should still try to be aware and understand what is happening. Take the game of fishing. We accept it as a sport. Though we know we are hurting the fish, we tend not to think too much about it. There is no awareness. If we are aware, we will think of the suffering of the fish. We will see that we are creating the cause for future suffering. The negative effect of killing the fish will for sure ripen one day even if it is not immediate. There will be suffering to bear. Suffering is obvious to us when it is physical pain, for example. But karma as the cause of suffering cannot readily be seen and often goes unnoticed. Even on the odd occasion that we happen to recognize that something is amiss, we may still dismiss it as part of normal, everyday life. We need to be aware that we are doing this.

We begin by trying to think and to reflect more carefully our conditions, both outer and inner. We are vigilant in our observations of people and their actions. We observe the effects and impact of people's actions on one another. This will in turn allow us to see beyond our norm. It may be unpleasant and disturbing at times, but it is not the seeing that is disturbing. We are just facing up to the conditions of *samsara* and karma as they are. The more we can see, the less our negativities (rooted in ignorance) can influence us. We will in turn have a little space where we can begin to appreciate that there is another way. We can wish for conditions to improve for everyone. This is actually one way of mind-training or practice.

When we first begin to practice, we naturally want to be peaceful. We want to feel nice. But we find that we are somewhat disturbed by the many things that are happening. Again we reflect on karma and the meaning of cause and effect. We will realize that only by our positive attitudes and actions will we achieve positive results. In general, we are happy when people do the right thing. Their positive behaviors do affect us emotionally. At times, we feel gratitude while at other times, we are inspired to reciprocate the caring or responsible behaviors. This is why in the practice of mind-training, to rejoice in the good deeds of others is an attitude that is much encouraged. Because a mind that rejoices at the merits of others is predisposed to acting beneficially for them.

Negative actions or experiences shouldn't be discarded as bad since they have the potential to bring us to the path of enlightened mind provided we can see and understand how they relate to the functioning of mind. Whenever we are faced with something disagreeable, it is not right for us to lose control and act as we please. It is not right to attack it, to complain, or to get frustrated and angry. Instead, we look within ourselves to try to understand our reaction. Why do we feel the dislike so much? We try to find answers about ourselves in the way we behave, talk, and communicate with others. Why do we always feel a little bit disturbed, or feel a little bit hurt? On the other hand, we cannot just cover up the unpleasantness by claiming that everything is nice, there is no problem, and then we can just let go. It is when we are distressed that we should take the opportunity to see all the aspects. We use the situation to help us reach a deeper understanding of our inner feelings and attitudes. This is also a form of mind-training that will facilitate our understanding of the conditions of *samsara*.

Whenever we engender *bodhicitta* in our thoughts and motivation, do something positive, or engage in Dharma practice, and we accumulate positive merits. In keeping with our original intent to help other people, it is natural for us to wish that our good merits and positive results likewise would go to benefit them. This is what it means to dedicate our positive merits to other sentient beings. The benefit of dedication is obviously twofold. It reduces our self-attachment and turns the mind towards others.

Very often we pressure ourselves to be perfect. We have this internal dialogue: *"I must do this, I did not do so well, I can't do it, or it's too difficult."* We should not follow such feelings. In our daily life, we function according to our capacity without giving in to undue pressure, obligation, or force of habit. Habitual tendencies are not negative per se but they still block us from being spontaneous (without being impulsive).

For now, we do what we can when we can. We try to understand the meaning of our thoughts, and actions. We also take the time to really reflect on how the Dharma teachings can apply to us. Without a careful evaluation of the validity of the teachings, we may just feel an obligation to do as we are told. Not understanding why, we will remain in our normal ways. We will not change. We may begin to harbor a few good wishes for others, which is still beneficial. However, the real value of the teachings will elude us. Check to see if the Dharma teachings can help you make sense of what is happening in your regular day. You will find that the more you check, the closer you will get to the meaning. The meaning will become clearer the more you analyze, and it will get easier. We should not dismiss, or ignore the teachings by branding them too difficult, or impossible. This kind of attitude is an obstacle. Very naturally one day, you will feel what the teachings mean to you. You will also understand what is beneficial to us all. Then spontaneously, you will be helpful to others.

ORIENTATION TO HELP

A caution worth noting is when we try to apply the enlightened attitude and help others, it does not mean we deliberately go to every individual and see how we can help. We should not think that we have to give the right message or that we have to help. This is, in fact, our holding on to an idea. Again, the idea is not as important as its meaning. The meaning is the real truth which shows a different way, different from our current way of thinking, acting, and being. This way is open to us.

We may identify who we are by the job we do, our role in the family, and/or our social status. You are *"so and so"* of a certain position, of some authority in an organization. If you identify the self with such roles, then you have lost sight of the meaning of who you are. By examining and applying the teachings, we can begin to clear up a lot of our questions and doubts particularly with respect to our attitudes and actions. Everything will then fall into place naturally. When we connect with the teachings, our path becomes very much like climbing a mountain. We know that the view from the top is very clear, and we will be able to see everything. But being at the foot of the mountain now, our view is blocked or fragmented. As we climb the mountain, we begin to see more and more. The more we apply and practice our understanding, the clearer we become. When we see clearly, we will know how to help. So how we can help becomes a question of how we can become clear about our conditions and the conditions around us. Only then can we become naturally helpful to others.

When we are able to connect our mind increasingly with a proper motivation grounded in *bodhicitta*, we can work with it. Very naturally, our speech, attitude, and actions will become more proper, and authentic. Otherwise, the enlightened attitude is just a good idea and it remains just an idea, that's all. It does not quite work for us. This is evident in our daily situations when we relate to our friends and families. We see everyone trying really his best, yet, things still don't seem to work out very well. There is something missing. This is the reason why there is so much confusion, and complications between people. Having good intentions, or good will is just not enough. If we cannot see clearly, we cannot know what is needed and helpful. This is why we have to be very clear first, then we will know what is important and beneficial for others.

We are always modeling after others, for example, we choose to dress in trendy colors and styles. We do it almost out of habit. Someone impresses you, and you try to imitate him. You never give any thought to his inner qualities. You follow in a somewhat superficial way. This does not mean that following a model is wrong either. By following the Dharma, we are encouraged to be ethical and to act positively thereby avoiding the causes of suffering. We should go deeper by examining what it is that we are actually following. And we will find that there is a way to clear and to free ourselves from the conditions of *samsara*. Little by little, we increase our understanding, and go deeper. Otherwise, we stay the same. There is no hurry. Hurrying to get the results is not right either. We should know that change takes time.

The word, illusion, is used to describe the condition that we are in. Illusion is a delicate word. To be more precise, it means that we are trapped by our superficial way of seeing. We cannot see deeper. For example, when we eat, we are caught up by the tastes of the spices. Flavors such as salty, sweet, or sour capture our taste buds. As a result, we don't really get to taste the natural flavors of the vegetables per se. But if we pay closer attention to what lies beneath all the seasonings, we will find that each vegetable has its own unique flavor, and texture. This is only one example. Similarly, when we are caught up in our illusion, we cannot go deeper. However, it does not mean that we have to think that our lives are an illusion, that nothing is real either. Everything is real to us now. This is reality to us. What it means is that we have to be aware of our conditions, and that it is possible to go deeper than what we are used to. We become clearer, and soon, we will see how things really are. As the saying goes, *"There is more than what meets the eye."* When we say the teachings are very deep, we don't mean that they are very complicated. They are simple but we have to see clearly.

All the explanations of the teachings are there to help us see clearly, to help us understand. They make it easier for us so we don't get stuck. They are informative so that we will know. When we know, we will not be trapped by our tendencies, and emotions anymore. Like the example of the taste of vegetables, do you know the real taste of carrots, or cabbage? We think we know, but perhaps we really don't know!

The same applies to our notion of "practice". We receive a lot of lectures and instructions so we have some ideas about it. But how do we make use of these ideas? We don't exactly know how. For example, the terms such as listening,

reflecting, or meditation all have been emphasized repeatedly. What does listening mean? We
know how to listen but sometimes we don't listen very well. We listen mixed with our tendencies. For instance, you are talking to someone
about gardening. He is explaining about the different kinds of flowers and describing the gardening techniques to you. Your understanding
necessarily comes from your experience of gardening – what you are used to. This is immediate. Most of the time, we think we know. But we
really know the concepts in a way that is familiar
to us, and so our knowing is limited by our
knowledge. As a result, we don't really listen
properly. But when we hear we also need to reflect, which is necessary to increase our understanding. In the teachings, it is described as
precise listening, precise looking, and precise
reading. It is possible when we are no longer
caught up in our usual tendencies and conditions.

To understand clearly is to make the mind
clear on the basic nature of a sentient being. We
are not so we say we are confused, we are
blocked. We are confused about the problems,
distractions, and even happiness. In other
words, we are confused about everything that
we experience now. This is why confused existence goes around in a circle as in *samsara*.

There is nothing miraculous about understanding clearly. It is possible for every one of
us to have this ability, this clarity of mind. The
challenges of daily life are relative. We just have
to work with them. The difficulty lies not out

there but inside of us. It comes from our tendencies linked to confusion in the mind and so we cannot see clearly. Things appear complicated, and we don't know what to do.

From a clear mind's perspective, everything is simple. The Buddha taught that we should be very simple. Some people misinterpret it as meaning we should give up everything, and not use the high-tech or modern implements of daily life. In fact, even if you give up everything, mind is still not simple. There is no way to be simple outwardly. When Buddha said we should be simple, it means that if we are very clear at an inner level, then everything becomes simple. Without the precise understanding, everything is complicated. So the Buddha said we must do the practice and be simple.

When we understand and see clearly, we are peaceful. Peaceful means not depending on others. We depend on ourselves. We could very well live somewhere by ourselves in solitude. But Mahayana[15] Buddhism teaches that we should not forget about others. Otherwise, we would not be able to attain a clear mind. It may sound strange, but it is actually very practical. Without fail, we go back to *bodhicitta*. When you sit alone and meditate quietly doing nothing, then

[15] "Mahayana (Sanskrit): "great vehicle". Mahayana is a particular form of Buddhism that employs the practice of skilful means (with great compassion as the method) and cultivates the wisdom that realizes the emptiness of self and all phenomena." – from Shamar Rinpoche, *The Path to Awakening, A Commentary on Ja Chekawa Yeshé Dorjé's Seven Points of Mind Training*: New Delhi, Motilal Barnasidass, 2009.

your mind is simple. Everything is simple. Moreover, you can achieve certain good results. But in order to be clearer, you need to be with people, to deal with them. "Dealing with people" in this context does not mean the normal way of working in the office with others. It means you have to be ethical in all situations. Doing so will in turn enhance your understanding. Meditation alone will not do it. It may appear as though there is a contradiction here. Actually, it makes sense. The purpose of the Buddhist path is to teach us how to work with oneself so as to help others. Through the practice, we may achieve some clarity; and unavoidably, it will have an influence in our daily life. We may also wish to apply what we have learnt. It does not work if we force or pressure ourselves to do it out of obligation. Therefore, we remain relaxed. We have the right intention, and then we wait for the right opportunity to put it into action. Even if we forget, it doesn't matter. There will always be other opportunities. We have the right intention already through the right understanding. When faced with a difficult situation, we will remember naturally. It is a mistake to try once, and when it doesn't work, we drop it. Again, there is no urgency. From time to time, when you see fit, you will apply the teachings appropriately. If you forcibly try to apply to just any situation, it will backfire and cause the tendencies to arise. The emotions will bring more confusion into the situation. Take your time and relax. Relax does not mean to not get involved, but to wait for the right moment.

One common problem is we don't want to take the time. As a result, things appear very complicated because we have not put in the time to understand properly in the first place. Sometimes, all we need is more time, clearer explanations, and better communication to clear up the confusion. But we just don't want to do it because we are reluctant to invest more time and the problem remains. It is like not taking the antidote so the poison remains. The tendencies and habits will always continue. This is an essential point. We must take the time. Therefore, as explained before, we listen, and we reflect properly. When you are working with your children, or people in general, try to pay attention and spend the time to listen and communicate properly. By doing so, you will avoid big problems and you will be able to solve them. The normal tendency is to not want to get involved in order to save time. This is how we are. Sometimes, it is because we really don't know how to help. But when we can help, we should take the time to do so. Otherwise, the problems will keep coming back. The teachings advise us to be patient and deal with the hassles and inconveniences. Only then will we be able to continuously put in the time and effort that will bring us the good results.

The Approach to Meditation

Meditation (*gom* in Tibetan) is the central practice of Buddhism. However, practitioners more often than not approach meditation looking to satisfy their personal interests, aims, and expectations. These usually detract from the original purpose of meditation making it difficult to achieve the results. Only when we know the aim and goal of meditation can we properly practice it. When we do, we will understand our own conditions and know how to make necessary adjustments along the way. Talking about meditation is easy. Everyone seems to agree that practice is a good thing yet we can't seem to actually commit to it. Individually, we somehow get sidetracked. This is human nature. There are always other things to pursue on life's agenda, and we don't really invest time and effort in meditative practice.

Sometimes Buddhism is regarded superficially as a religion, a philosophy, or a discipline.

Unfortunately, lost is the essential goal of Buddhism – to live an ethical and meaningful life adept at achieving beneficial results for sentient beings. All Dharma teachings converge on this one essential goal. A genuine aspiration towards this goal is like a seed which will grow into a tree of realization bearing the fruit of Buddhahood.

For now, due to the veils of mind, we can only continue along the same worldly way, which appear complicated and problematic. We also tend to wait for someone else to take care of us and our responsibilities rather than getting clear ourselves and solving our own problems. While we wait, we achieve nothing. If we put in the effort and really work with our understanding, there is no doubt we will achieve results. Why we would rather defer to someone else to help us is due to our fear, a little laziness on our part, and a slight reluctance to get involved. If you watch carefully, you will see these conditions are there and they immobilize you to some degree. We should try to understand why some life situations are difficult for us. If we look carefully, we may find that our effort is lacking, or we lack confidence or "know how". We all have problems and we don't like them. At times, even when we know how to solve a problem, we feel no immediacy to act on it because we lack courage. Our hesitation blocks us. This is how we are in life situations in general and we are the same when it comes to the Dharma. The Dharma is actually much easier. There is not so much to learn and study as in academia or the professions. Yet, the result of Dharma practice will undoubtedly enable you to function better in normal life and bring much benefit to you and those around you. The Dharma is therefore well worth our real commitment.

REFUGE AND BODHICITTA ARE PREREQUISITES

The teachings stress that meditation and any Buddhist practice must be connected to the meaning of Refuge and *bodhicitta*. *Bodhicitta*, the enlightened attitude is easier to understand though more difficult to implement. Refuge is more complicated. Its exact meaning is harder to get. Nevertheless, we try to reflect carefully. The taking of Refuge is not only a formal ceremony marking the entrance to the Buddhist path, it is in fact a connection to the Buddha, Dharma, and Sangha. Implicit in our taking Refuge is that we have chosen to establish this connection. A deeper meaning of Refuge is to aim to understand and accept the meaning of the teachings of the Buddha. The image of Dharma is represented by Buddhist texts. But its real meaning comes through in the way it affects us in our actions and who we are. To take Refuge in the Dharma is to be protected by the meaning of the Buddha's teachings. The problem is its application is lacking because we always forget to connect it to our daily life. When our thinking and actions are congruous with the Dharma, we are protected from wrongdoings and negative results in this and future lives. Nowadays, people take Refuge for different reasons. Some people are not particularly dissatisfied with their lives but they feel something is missing. Some may have a need to understand a certain suffering. Others have trouble dealing with people because of hatred, aggression, or anger. All these are problems inherent in being human. The one basic reason for everyone to seek answers is, *"I want to know."* The Buddha gave the Dharma teachings to give us what we need, and it is a path to arrive at a clear and true understanding.

The understanding of *bodhicitta* is a pre-requisite to understanding the meaning of Dharma. If we don't understand *bodhicitta*, or if we are unable to work with it, then there will be gaps in our understanding. *Bodhicitta* always links self to others. You can take Refuge thinking only of yourself but you will encounter roadblocks ahead. In other words, you will be handicapped.

Gampopa emphasized that Dharma was the proper path and that any progress on the path would be dependent on *bodhicitta*. The enlightened attitude is the wish for everyone to be free from suffering. People in general want to know how to find relief from suffering, how to avoid it. In this context, suffering is more than physical pain. It includes all forms of suffering connected to the general conditions of life, and individual experiences. The question is how to avoid suffering. Many methods and explanations are there to help us but they all boil down to the right understanding of the essential points of Dharma. Then, everything will go smoothly. Otherwise, we remain caught up in the cycle – it means that you are engaged to life's conditions through your attachments and expectations and you perpetuate the cycle of wanting and the inevitability of suffering.

To put it simply, I have a problem and I want to solve it. My mind has to be clear first so I do the practice. Then after a little while, I notice that even with all the methods available to me, somehow, I am unable to solve my basic problem. I practice for a long time, and there is a little improvement. There is some result, but I am still not free. The problem remains. Then the answer will come – I have to engender *bodhicitta*. Without it, I cannot be rid of my problem. If I am honest with myself, I will see that it is my self-clinging that prevents me from seeing perfectly everything as it is. To understand self-clinging, I have to connect with the Dharma. The Buddha explained that due to ignorance in the mind, it puts me in the wrong way creating ever more problems. By understanding that I have the same root problem of mind as everybody else, my attitude will begin to shift towards a non-differentiation between self and others. Knowing that my problem is universally experienced, I will feel more inclined to help others. While engendering this more caring and sympathetic attitude towards others, I search for a way out. I find the solution in the Dharma so I commit to learning and practicing it.

When the non-differentiation between self and others becomes apparent to you, you will start to see everything. When you feel that you can do something good for others, things start to work somehow. This feeling is your basic nature. You have to feel it for it to work. It will not work if you simply think you have to help others first in order to solve your own problems. You have to really care for the needs of others. This is the key difference in attitude and motivation. If you see a big problem for others, and you really want to help, this attitude helps your own mind. If I help others in order to help myself, it does not quite work. This difference is so easily and often mistaken. The altruistic attitude is spontaneous and natural. Therefore, when we engage in *bodhicitta*, we are at once clear and caring about the needs of others. The result according to karma is we accumulate merits so that we can see in proper perspective. Then, it is up to us to think and act according to our capacity.

We should pay attention to discriminating thoughts such as, *"I like this, I don't like that."* Try to be more neutral and "equal" in the way we relate to different people and things in general. The opposite of seeing sameness among people's conditions is to discriminate. Be aware when you harbor thoughts such as, *"He is a bad person. He should suffer."* There is usually some contradiction in mind that pulls away from *bodhicitta*. Therefore consider it more carefully and the answers will come. If we try to see things just logically, then there will be judging. We will see faults, mistakes and many other things will follow. For that reason, we need to see clearly that everyone is under the same conditions which help us to engender *bodhicitta*. When we do, we will help others and in turn we develop our *bodhicitta* capacity. We all have the potential to understand this sameness. We all have *bodhicitta* in our nature. In one way, there is no need to develop its qualities. If we really try to see, we will know that we do have this capacity.

Embracing *bodhicitta* does not mean we have to like everyone. The essential point is to see the sameness in conditions for all of us. This acknowledgement or discovery opens our mind. It is very difficult to like everyone which is not the point here. Take a person who likes birds but is afraid of insects. This discrimination in his mind makes him help only birds and not the insects. He cannot understand why he should help insects. This kind of discrimination applies to people as well, *"I like this person but I hate that person."* Of course, even if we try to change, we cannot do it. Again, it goes back to seeing the basic conditions of every being as universal and the same. Only then are we able to understand what is important. When we can see more equally and that the difficulties are common to all, then even when it comes to someone we don't like, we will still help. Our help is given without any conditions and without any expectations in return. This then is *bodhicitta* working properly with the right understanding.

Due to the obscurations of mind, we cannot see the conditions. Take the same example of disliking insects, if we really analyze our aversion, we will find no reason to hate them. We don't need to keep them in the house either. We can take them outside. This is normal. You don't need to hate them nor consider them as a problem. It is natural not to want them in your room. By bringing them outside, you don't lose *bodhicitta*. This is just an example. Whenever you don't like something or someone, it is your concept. If you reflect carefully on it, you will find that it is not important. Take the time to examine a condition or concept when it appears in mind, and it will dissolve. Mind will be clear again. In the teachings, a common analogy used to describe this process is: when the clouds dissipate, the sun is there. The clouds *"clear"* by themselves, and the sky is clear. When we are prejudiced against a spider, for instance, we think it ugly, dangerous and poisonous. But if we can understand a spider's natural conditions, then we can accommodate the fact that an insect has a form different from ours. Once again we don't have to like it but we can appreciate the fact that it has a mind and it, too, desires to live. Then, you don't wish to hurt it anymore. You may even wish to help it. This is how a different understanding about spiders can equalize or neutralize the original discrimination against it. Gone are the anger, aversion, and aggression towards it. Moreover, our mind is pacified. And we try to gain the same shift in understanding towards our fellow humans. We don't like everybody. This is natural, but we can understand that we each have the same nature and subject to the same conditions. This affords our mind some freedom or liberation from ignorance. The understanding makes the mind clearer so we can then reflect on the different conditions. Gradually, everything will appear clearer and we will be able to adjust accordingly.

Bodhicitta is not learnt through any special means. The many life-situations afford us opportunities to clearly understand it. It will come quite naturally when we practice. Try to be natural and there will be fewer problems and we can practice continuously. Whatever practice we are doing, meditation or another practice, when we know our main purpose is to help others including the self, then it means we have realization. It is a clear inner understanding that comes through the practice very spontaneously. Until that happens, there is usually a tiny gap in our understanding of *bodhicitta*. It is not difficult to overcome this gap but it takes time.

The bodhisattvas have developed the capacity of clarity very well. We also have this potential. We say they have a strong mind and they seem capable, energetic, and joyful. Of course, it is not easy to achieve this state of mind. This is why it is important to get the proper meaning of *bodhicitta* and try to stay connected to it. Then our mind can be clearer rather than confused. The problems are still there but we have found a way to deal with them. They no longer control us so we don't have to suffer them anymore.

THE SUPPORTS OF MEDITATION

There are many forms of meditation. Meditation means to keep the mind in equilibrium which means in balance. It is the one method that will yield the realization of awakened mind. To be successful in meditation requires a combination of conditions. As explained already, we have to prepare. We must go beyond a theoretical understanding. We must also be prepared to step out of our norm, to try to live and practice with more clarity and precision. We approach meditation with the right attitude and expectations.

To help the practitioners, realized masters in the past, both in India and Tibet, designed simple meditation practices. *"Simple"* in this context, does not mean quick and easy, as in the push of a button. *"Simple"* means that the methods have been designed in such a way that the essential points are combined together for us. It is up to us then to take the time to learn the methods, their meanings, and apply them in practice. When we do, our understanding will no longer be superficial. Doubts, criticisms, and expectations that can delay our progress will lessen. Real understanding will produce quick results for us.

People who wish to achieve results like the great masters did in the past should not rush. *"To rush"* is normal for us. We are always doing things expecting things to go smoothly and to get quick results. At the same time, we don't want to be a hamster in its running wheel, going very quickly, yet not going anywhere. The great lamas might use different examples but they always come to this point: when you sit, try to be aware of what you are doing. Sometimes, you are in a hurry to get a result repeating the same thing over and over again. Try to be aware when this happens to you.

To get a point *"precisely"* takes a long time yet it is essential that we do. It is the only way for us to change. When we have a serious illness, we have to seek a cure that can uproot the source of the problem, not only to temporarily relieve the symptoms. It is more than using a painkiller to ease the pain. Moreover, we may have to take the right medicine for a long time. The right medicine may not bring quick results, but over time, it cures the disease without producing harmful side effects. Slowly but surely, one's health will improve. A truly effective treatment restores one's health to its original condition. Similarly, when we practice meditation, we want to do it without creating side effects. We may think the quick practices are very powerful yet there might be some side effects if we have neglected to do the proper preparations. We don't have to be scared away either. It is just that when we know, then we can be careful. Vajrayana, which will be discussed later in the book, is not a path where the results are always immediate. There is no urgency so we don't have to put so much pressure in getting the results. The understanding will come gradually, slowly. It is also not necessary to try to avoid things, or to act in a very guarded and measured way. Rather, we do the practice, and we are careful. This approach actually applies to everything we do. Whether it is to improve our health, our actions, our practice, or our state of mind, the process is the same. We go step by step, taking care along the way.

With respect to the practice, certain points are always important to note. The teachings refer to them as a form of discipline. In this context, discipline does not mean control, or its usual meaning of following a code of behavior. Discipline keeps us connected to the qualities of the lineage masters. Discipline is needed because there is a boundary that we don't cross and it is the Dharma principles that keep us in line. The Dharma gives us guidelines which form an important basis for our actions and behavior so we don't act negatively. The teachings always remind us to be natural and spontaneous. It does not mean we simply let things happen either. On the contrary, when we are connected to the Dharma through proper understanding, we don't lose sight of it. In daily life, we make adjustments dealing with things that matter to us or don't, connected to the guidelines. We know what our capacity is, what we can do, and what we cannot. Gradually we develop ourselves. In this way, everything comes easily, naturally, and spontaneously in whatever we do.

The teachings give many points. You need to examine them, and you will have many questions. The questions will lead to clarification of your understanding. Generally, we hear something and we think we know it, we feel we understand it. We are always thinking, *"I've heard this before, or I think it's like this."* We tend to jump to conclusions and they remain unchallenged. Later, when we are presented with new information, we then realize that we didn't really get the point the first time around. So for now, we are not very clear, we are a little confused. But if we take the time and the effort to reflect more carefully, we can get a more precise understanding and clear up the confusion.

Especially with the Dharma, we really need to combine theory with actual meditative practice. It is through practical application that the questions arise that enable us to seek further clarification. This process can be seen in debates, which is a method of learning for Buddhist students in Himalayan countries. A debate is actually a series of questions and answers to gain greater clarity on an issue. In order to debate, one has to be clear about a number of points. During the debate, the points undergo scrutiny by logical arguments. This process in itself increases one's capacity to think clearly and results in a clearer mind.

Look in the biographies of the past masters, and you will find many examples of how the masters clarified their minds through their questioning, again and again. We should follow their example. Sometimes, as you read about the past masters, you may feel that it is not applicable to you, whether this feeling is conscious, or not, it is there. We have this conditioning in us where we think that we are not like the very important people. This attitude will deter us from reaching the correct understanding. Instead, we should analyze to see if we can integrate what we have read into our own lives. Of course, the reading still gives us concepts only, but nevertheless, those concepts can generate the important points, which can help us in our meditation. This is why it is worth our while to research on how the masters practiced, what were the main points they emphasized. We will then realize what is important for us, too. We check to see if we are integrating the essential points into our practice.

Following the Dharma path enables us to clear away our tendencies, and obscurations. Our tendencies are very subtle and difficult to see by ourselves. As we read the biographies of the masters, we try to go a little deeper, because there are many steps to discover. We tend to get caught up fascinated about the details of the feats and trials the masters had to go through. We think them wonderful, and so interesting. It is of course good to be impressed, but unfortunately, we stop there. We should question the reason behind each action, the essential point that was revealed in the narration: what were the conditions, the connections the masters made, and what were the significant results that followed? These biographies are thus an important source of knowledge. If we pay careful attention, then all the details and points will come our way. We need to gain and develop these crucial insights. When we do, our attitudes and orientation will inevitably change for the better. As mentioned before, we need discipline to help us stay connected to the Dharma's essential meanings, which reinforces the importance of discipline. Otherwise, everything is just reduced to rules and regulations, customs and obligation which we follow mechanically.

The Dharma is our guide. We always feel we have to have time, and follow certain ways but the essential points are our reference points. Once we know them, we will know how to be careful, how to use them. Results will develop and we will know how to attain enlightenment. The alternative is to remain in our habitual ways. It is up to us to really become clear about the meanings by our own reflection and application. This is the condition that will prepare us for practice and make it easy to do. We will know how much time to spend, which direction to go and what to look out for.

We are generally too fixed. This tendency is usually related to desire and attachment, so we are blocked. The teachings tell us that things are interrelated. For example, in order to realize our true nature, we have to be liberated from ignorance. And ignorance is the cause of suffering. In order to be liberated from the suffering, then we have to orient our mind differently. In order to have a proper orientation, the mind should not be blocked by our grasping. Grasping is of course difficult to break since it is a deep habit of mind. Due to the interrelatedness of things, following this basic grasping, tendencies continue to form and grow stronger. Even how we relate to the teachings is a form of grasping. It is difficult to let go.

The way to approach grasping is to keep the mind stable. Then we will know at some point what it means to grasp and how to be free from it. The degree of difficulty also varies between individuals. Some people can get the point right away, while others may struggle with it. Some may think it easy but doing it is rather difficult. Regardless of individual differences, the key is to *"take it easy."* This means no-grasping. Grasping is there whenever we feel something is too complicated or too difficult. Yet we don't want to be careless, or to simply let go. We want to be in equilibrium. Take meditation for example, when we meditate, we just do it, and it is all right. Then later on, we can make corrections or adjustments. But if we grasp during meditation, the mistakes will follow. Even when you are meditating well but if you cling to the progress, that is again a mistake. Therefore, try to let the mind be in an even and balanced way.

We might think: *"Oh, this is an illusion so I wish to get rid of it."* But that's not how it works. Until we reach the state of a Buddha, the illusion caused by ignorance is our state of mind. As we discover and understand more about our basic nature, the illusion will gradually dissipate by itself. All teachings point to the fact that the cause of suffering, and the conditions of *samsara* provide the basic means or opportunity to understand mind. Through the examining of our own conditions, our mind will start to develop more clarity. This development is not something that we can actually feel as in feeling that the ignorance is decreasing, or there is more clarity in the mind, or that the illusion is diminishing. We cannot feel the improvement. Rather, the improved clarity affects how we function.

When we begin to discover about ourselves,

we don't really change immediately in any noticeable way even though our understanding is actually improving. Because we can't see the result, we often feel that the practice is difficult. It is very different from everyday life where our work produces noticeable and relatively quick results. To understand the mind, we must not expect results that are detectable or immediate.

The conditions of our lives are very useful to us individually. They are like a resource to garner understanding. Each person's conditions are unique. Relative life, karma, and the capacity to understand differ between individuals. Karma is not fixed, nor is it definite. But the teachings lead us all towards the same direction. Therefore, we adjust our lives accordingly keeping with the Dharma. We adapt and change with awareness. We always want to be aware. Sometimes, we have to be more flexible, yet at other times, too much flexibility might give way to carelessness. If we are too tight, there is no space. Being flexible in a balanced way will enable us to work with the difficulties. These words may sound simple but you should really try to do it, to develop yourself in this way. Reflect on the deeper meaning of the teachings, the principles, and by connecting the dots by yourself, you will develop another way. This means you will be able to see the conditions in a clearer way anytime. You are beginning to recognize by yourself. You can practice all the time. Each instant, situation, or state of mind is important. Everything becomes the basis for recognizing mind.

In order to gain certainty about the true nature of human mind, we work on ourselves. We rely on Refuge, *bodhicitta* and meditation. By understanding the nature of conceptual thinking, of sentient beings and all conditions, everything becomes clear. The way to this understanding is through meditation, and a clear mind. Meditation is more than just a technique to achieve a result. Buddhist meditation leads to the understanding of the nature of self and others which will eventually lead to the recognition of the ultimate truth. This is the basic theory. The process is as explained already, to bring all the points together in order to get at the exact and precise meaning. We try to understand and reflect carefully on everything that has to do with the self and others to get at the precise meaning of the Dharma. Everything is an opportunity to lead to a clear mind without blockage.

The chief method is meditation. In our daily life, we try to use all the conditions that come our way. Good or bad, we use all situations to gain greater understanding. This does not mean we have to be constantly on the look out. When something appears, we are aware and use it accordingly. Because everything can be used, we can relax. In general, our mind is a little confused, and we feel pressured. We feel nervous, distracted, and not very happy. Things seem unpredictable and very unstable. How we feel often influence, or color our experience to some degree. But when we are clear about our own inner mental conditions, they are no longer problematic. Seeing them clearly, they neither disturb nor distract us. There is no negativity. For example, you feel angry. You are aware of it but you don't react to it negatively by lashing out at people. You are simply aware of your anger without acting under its influence. This means your mind is becoming clearer. Without the influence of the emotions, the many life situations become easier to handle. Your actions will be more appropriate and precise. You will be able to help others in a more effective way. This is a natural way to develop a clear mind without any force.

Meditation

Meditation enables the mind to remain in its own natural condition. "Natural", in this context, means to be in the present moment. The natural condition of mind refers to its essence, its nature, which is clear.

We say the nature of mind is lucid or light. But it is not light as in ordinary light from the sun, or light from a light bulb. "Light" means very clear. We always mistakenly think that when we meditate, some light, or something clear will appear to us. It is important not to be caught up by the term. When you do the practice, you will come to its true meaning. If we are trapped by a concept, it may cause some confusion because we tend to follow what we think. Sometimes we may think we are clear when we are not. That error actually clouds the mind. All the terms such as lucid, clear light, or enlightenment connote "light" – as in a shiny crystal that reflects light quite naturally.

The opposite of clear is unclear. "Unclear" means that when we sit, we have a lot of thoughts. There is a meditation called *zhine*, in Tibetan, or calm abiding, which means to be able to stay in a peaceful state of mind. *Zhine* pacifies the mind where thoughts are calmed and cleared away by themselves so the mind is clear.

Obscurations cover the true nature of mind. Our thoughts obscure our view like vapor on a crystal ball making it unreflective. The obscurations in the mind are caused by ignorance. Some people think that ignorance means a very dark state that is negative. Ignorance is not like that at all. You could have many clever ideas and thoughts but at the same time, ignorance is there. Though the nature of mind is clear, at the same time, the obscurations are there, like the vapor on the crystal. They are caused by emotional afflictions, conceptual knowledge, and habits as explained already[16].

When you meditate, try to orient your mind towards the natural state. Try to become clear of your own conditions, and how your mind is functioning. You have learnt the meaning of mind in its natural state and its obscurations, you can. It is in your meditation that some feeling of the actual meaning will slowly appear to you.

Meditation is a method to help the mind to become clear. At the moment, even when we are quite smart, our mind is still somewhat clouded.

----

[16] See chapter 2.

Mind is always following something. Mind cannot settle or get centered. The conditions are always with us. This is why in the beginning, we need to really apply ourselves to meditation. We have to work at our concentration. Without it, our mind is unclear and we are overcome by distractions and drowsiness.

Meditation can help to reverse our habitual state of mind, and bring about mind's natural capacity. Since mind is present and clear, it is able to work with the present moment. By practicing consistently, being present in the moment becomes a habit. We will see the problems and situations clearly. We will know how to solve problems such as fear, depression, and confusion. Because our perspective of any problem, big or small, depends on our attitudes and character, when we can see clearly our inner conditions, then we will know what to do. We will be free. This is the main goal of meditation.

We have to learn meditation step by step just like everything else. Learn how our mind functions then everything becomes simple. The deep understanding gained in meditation is quite different from knowledge in the normal worldly sense. We call it realization. It is an understanding that comes from our own mind about our own mind. We cannot buy it. We cannot get it somewhere outside of us. Because we can achieve this realization of mind, it is said that the human life is precious.

Theoretically, in order to understand mind, we have to know very precisely the characteristics of mind. For example, emptiness is a quality of mind. Often our idea about the term is wrong. Yet emptiness can only be realized through an in-depth research into mind linked with meditation. We progress steadily by our inner examinations and analyses. It is a long process. Analysis does not involve making up anything. Nothing is fabricated. However, there is a system that we can follow to attain realization. This is similar to the learning of a science where one progresses through a series of courses, learning step by step. It is risky to just talk about emptiness or realization. We have to actually reach an understanding by ourselves. Now, we are searching what it is that is mind. Once we do have realization, it is no longer a passing thing subject to change. The realization of mind is mind.

In meditation we allow the mind to be flexible which will bring about some understanding. If we are stuck in the words and terminology of the instructions then we cannot gain a deeper understanding. We have Buddha-nature – the potential to realize mind's nature. "Buddha" means the accomplishment of a clear mind. We have to put in the effort, all the more during the meditation sessions, we try to keep the awareness of a clear mind. We don't cling to the concepts or ideas of what meditation should be. Otherwise, we will get stuck again. We allow the mind to improve by itself. To improve, we always follow the meditation instructions. These are usually written down with examples to illustrate their meaning. Milarepa (1052-1135) composed many songs to remind himself of the key points. We can prepare ourselves by studying and learning the meaning of the songs to gain an approach in mind-training.

Whenever we are meditating, watching or analyzing our mind, there is a kind of grasping going on yet we don't want to grasp. All the teachings tell us not to. So we have to first understand what does it mean to grasp? We always think that in order to get anything done, we have to grasp. This is truly how we feel. We may understand the words, "no grasping," but we can't do it. We cannot help but grasp. By following precisely the Buddha's methods, whether there is grasping or not, you will still achieve the results. Perhaps the results will be even better without grasping. Where there is less grasping, there is less suffering also. Even if we can't do it immediately, having an intellectual understanding for now is still a very good starting point.

When we try to find the meaning of grasping, to see the object of grasping, the effect of grasping, and so on, and we go about our investigation as such, we will find that to become naturally free of grasping is a very, very slow process. Meditation, however, is simply just sit and be aware. Moreover, when we look we will see all kinds of negative emotions such as jealousy, pride, and attachment. If we push ourselves to get clear of them we are in fact again grasping for a state without emotions. The point therefore is not to avoid grasping, or not to be rid of it. The point is to be aware of the grasping and we will understand it. Meditation is the method to make us aware, and to keep our mind in equanimity, in balance. There should not be any pressure applied and at the same time there is no wanting. This sounds easy enough but it is very difficult to do. So, we continue to encourage ourselves and we remember what the teachings tell us.

If we try to see the results of meditation, it could get complicated. If we say to meditate means to be very clear about mind's nature, this does not quite work because we will look and try to grasp what that nature is. So the teachings on meditation often explain it like this, "to meditate means there is nothing to meditate on, and there is no holding on to a self." Calling it "no-meditation" or "non-meditation" also does not work. So meditation means the absence of holding on to a self, thoughts and actions. Just sit. It does not feel like meditating at all.

When we sit, we need to bring the meaning of the teachings we have studied into the practice. Meditation is just a term. We use awareness, the condition of meditation. If we just sit, it will not fetch any significant results, maybe some effects over time. Apply the teachings to the practice itself, then you will know what is necessary and what is important for you. We can actually gain a direct feeling, or experience of what the teachings mean. Meditation can be difficult when we are not used to it. It is difficult to understand how it is done. But try to practice from time to time without expecting anything, just look very clearly, then more and more we will understand by ourselves. We will need to make use of many situations or problems in order to expand this understanding and to gradually clarify the mind.

From time to time, as you sit, you may feel an instant of peace. You can't create it but it's there, and it's very clear. It may last less than a second. This is normal for someone who is not used to it. It appears then it is gone again. This kind of experience can happen many times. It is a glimpse into the natural peace of mind. Even when we are very tired, we sit down, and it appears. Or in the middle of doing something, we take a break, and it appears. It feels nice. We don't know what it is and sometimes, we don't even notice it.

The problem is our constant evaluation of everything, whether it is good or bad. Even when we are in a peaceful state, we compare it or try to see if it fits one of our familiar experiences and habits and the peace disappears. We always feel that we have to do something with it, or we follow it, and it disappears. Due to a lack of familiarity or recognition, we often miss it and it passes. Many methods exist to enable the practitioner to catch or recognize it. Meditation is such a method. Again, don't get caught up in the concept of meditation; rather, stay in the natural state of mind. In this way, we will be able to develop the peace of mind.

The first step in meditation is to calm the mind. We let our mind become clear naturally without fabrication, making room for clarity to appear. We do have to develop the calm but not by force. We can't make it happen. At times, we feel a contradiction. The instructions tell us to be very natural, yet our mind has to focus. We feel the two are contradictory. Actually they are not. By focusing our mind, we will come to understand mind's essence. It is difficult to describe the essence of mind because words can confuse us.

First, we learn the theory of meditation. In a way, the theory is very simple but we still have to learn it. We should neither think it difficult nor easy. We have to go through the practice. In the beginning, we learn how to be quiet in body and mind. Of course, silence in speech is automatic when we are not talking. So we just sit and remain quiet.

We want to be relaxed, but how do we relax? We cannot relax when we are agitated, or thinking too much. We have to learn to relax. Everyone is different. But the most common way to relax is to sit quietly for short periods of time. First, just have this idea in mind. We are always pushing ourselves going from one thing to the next. We feel as if we have to be occupied, so we cannot relax. We are always in this mode. So here, the idea is to sit for short periods of time. We decide that we are going to do this. When we do, we will naturally feel more able to do so, more released from the pressure to do something in the next moment. This enables us to relax. It is not as easy as it seems, of course, but it is a start in the right direction.

To relax does not only mean in the physical posture of sitting. The thinking also has to relax, otherwise, it is very difficult to meditate. But we start by learning how to sit quietly, in a relaxed way. It makes it easier to apply the methods of meditation. It's easier for people who don't have a lot to do to relax. People who are always very busy with many responsibilities will find it harder to relax even for a few minutes. When they sit quietly, they are still thinking incessantly. It is good for them to adopt the attitude that they will take the time to relax. This attitude will slowly enable them to do it.

We try to be clear while relaxed. Two conditions can hinder our progress – mental distractions and drowsiness. Mental distractions or wanderings include personal thoughts of all kinds such as good ideas, pleasant anecdotes, and recalls. As the wandering continues, mind is distracted so there is no clarity. Drowsiness can sometimes be pleasant or not depending on whether the mind is relaxed or tired. Because our habits of mind are strong, we must be aware of these two disruptions to meditation so we can stay relaxed. Sometimes, the mind is not thinking as much so it is relaxed and it stays. This kind of mind can appear to us outside of meditation, for instance, when we are tired and we are just resting.

Even before the meditation, we should already try to relax, try to apply the skill to relax. You will know exactly what this means when you do it. Practice lets us discover another way. We may be very busy in our daily life with many conditions that require our attention such as our jobs, family, and relationships. We should keep these obligations separate. For instance, you work at the office and you look after your family when you're home. Home and office should be kept separate. Don't bring your work home and vice versa. Otherwise, the office problem gets dragged home causing problems there as well. The original problem multiplies, and before you know it, you have problems everywhere. Take a breather when you get home, or when you arrive at the office. This helps you to cope with more awareness. It will help your relaxation during meditation. Habits, negative emotions, and tendencies make our mind heavy. When we can relax, they become more apparent to us. We can then understand that there is an alternative way. Each of us will develop gradually towards it according to our individual needs.

The teachings can provide explanations for the different types of mental states, but they can't prescribe an exact formula for an individual. In any case, we don't want to be controlled by instructions either. The teachings give us guidelines and explanations. It is up to us individually to discover what the teachings are really pointing to – the conditions of our own mind. Then we will know clearly what to do, what is beneficial and what is not, how to function in daily life. This again is the goal of taking refuge in the Dharma.

We will see how some ways are good yet difficult to follow. Some ways are harmful but we can't change due to strong habits. How can we change then? As explained before, we have to keep questioning to get at the answers to become clearer. Simply following our own ideas and meditating will not bring about clarity.

However, if we honestly engage in our quest to understand, the questions will come up and guide us along. We will see for ourselves that the obscurations caused by the habitual tendencies are indeed strong. To deal with them, we always begin with relaxing the mind.

Meditation explores the functioning of the mind. There are two conditions of mind known as *nepa* and *gyurwa* in Tibetan. *Nepa* means a stable mind undisturbed by thoughts. In the beginning, this stable mind may last only a few seconds. Gradually, as you get used to it, you will be able to stay with it for longer periods. *Gyurwa* refers to the coming and going of thoughts in the mind. One thought leads to another so we say there is a constant stream of changing thoughts. A new thought automatically infers a change. When your mind is stable, the change appears quicker. Because you are aware, you will feel the thoughts moving more quickly. If you are caught up in the thoughts, it means you are no longer aware of them. As soon as you are aware of the thoughts, they dissolve on their own. One after another, the thoughts will fall away, non-stop like sheets of rain.

Rikpa allows us to understand our own mind. *Rikpa* means clear mind, clear awareness. It recognizes *nepa* and *gyurwa*. The absence of *rikpa* means we are not conscious of our thought flow so we are carried along by it. To be aware of thoughts in *nepa* requires a presence of mind that sees what's going on called mindfulness (*drenpa* in Tibetan), a level of mind that can see everything, all the conditions.

Another important capacity is mindful awareness (*shezhin* in Tibetan). It is a form of *rikpa*. It means that we are clear and aware of what is happening so that we can make adjustments. It is therefore a clearer state than just being present. Again, these terms introduce meditation to the practitioners. Meditators who are used to the practice can get these points easily. But for beginners, it is difficult to get the precise meanings. Nevertheless, it is helpful to familiarize with the meaning of these terms because they are the conditions of meditation.

In order to help the beginner, supports for meditation are recommended. Support means help, or aid for the principal focus which is the condition of meditation itself. An example of one support is the breath. Through observing the breath, we can see whether the mind is calm or agitated. We leave the mind in its natural state without changing it. We are aware of the in- and out-breaths. Some practitioners are advised to count them up to 21 times without being distracted from the count. The important point is to be able to maintain awareness throughout the counting. This means to be aware of each in- and out-breath. When we are aware of the breath, any thought that appears will also disappear of its own accord. Another thought may then appear. Again, it is *nepa* that remains conscious of the counting, and the breaths. *Gyurwa*, which means change, will sometimes cause us to lose consciousness of counting when we follow other thoughts. For example, you are distracted when the counting reaches ten. The next count to eleven is no longer a conscious act. But immediately, *rikpa* or *shezhin* will allow you to understand what is happening - that you have strayed from counting. You will know to return the mind to counting. The counting mind is focusing on the counting and the breathing. Each serves as a support so that we know when we are distracted. If you try to simply focus on your own functioning of mind, you will find it extremely difficult and complicated. It is far easier to use a support such as the counting of breaths. Missing a few counts is not detrimental. The important point is to always bring your attention back when it has strayed which is basic to meditation. Gradually, your mind will be able to stay with the awareness for longer and longer periods.

Methods are actually supports for meditation. Support means to make it easier to meditate. Therefore, we should neither fixate on the support nor pressure ourselves to follow it strictly. The supports are there only to enable the mind to come to a balanced state, a state of equilibrium. Again, we fall back on proper understanding. We have to be clear about what we are doing so the practice becomes simple.

By learning how to sit, how to relax, and how to see all the conditions of mind, we are in effect training our mind. To train implies that we already have the potential or capacity, which until now has not been developed. We have the potential to meditate, we just need to do it. We don't grasp at what we are doing. We sit and really go through the practice. Any condition that comes our way during the sitting meditation or in our daily life, we use it to gain further understanding. We apply the same awareness and method of thinking introspectively in all situations. It is quite difficult to do immediately without some training first. You have to get used to it.

A basic principle is to be more open. Sometimes, you may feel that sitting meditation and daily life are two different and separate situations. When you sit, you think that you have to sit like this and focus like that. You feel that it is so important. Afterwards, you don't apply yourself in the same way during free time or during the normal course of the day. "Free" in this context means outside the meditation session. This kind of attitude can in fact block you. The point is to be open and aware at all times. We must understand that meditation is to develop a clear mind so we can understand mind itself which is with us all the time.

When you practice, you will have many questions as to how to be clear. The clarity of mind is developed by clearing up the obscurations through meditation. First, we apply the methods to reach a stable mind. There are two aspects to stability: how to become stable, and then how to improve it. Due to the natural law of cause and effect, conditions may be present in you that prevent you from attaining stability or deter you from further progress. In the midst of adverse conditions, the very effective practices and teachings of the Vajrayana can help you to change those conditions. In general, Vajrayana

practices are helpful to everyone without discrimination. At the same time, they can meet
the specific needs, characteristics and circumstances of the individual. If you want to recover
from an illness, you must take the specific remedy for your condition and not somebody else's
condition. But more importantly, how well Vajrayana practices can work for you depends on
your efforts, and the depth of your commitment.

A Glimpse of Vajrayana

Buddhism offers different approaches to meditative practices such as the paths of Hinayana, Mahayana, and Vajrayana (included in the Mahayana path). These are not three separate categories of paths or practices; rather, the distinctions are reflective of the practitioners' personal attitudes and individual capacity. The Vajrayana path leads to the understanding of mind. It is not an academic discipline one pursues in school. There are no passing grades, no start or finish. Vajrayana may come natural to some people and difficult for others. It depends on one's inner capacity, propensity and personality. Some people may find that Vajrayana does not suit them. This in no way infers that their capacity is blocked. It just means that now is not the right time. They may decide later.

The precise meaning of Vajrayana may well elude many people. Vajrayana concepts and methods sound exciting and intriguing. However, the connection to the essence of Vajrayana is not possible by just following instructions. The meanings are not obvious nor can they be easily explained. They go much deeper than words can convey. Unlike the instructions to connect some electronic equipment, for instance, Vajrayana teachings are much more than step-by step explanations, or systems of theories. Underlying the instructions and methods is the line of transmissions that we call lineage. The transmissions have been upheld and passed down unbroken, from master to disciple, through the generations until the present time. It is vital to maintain the purity of the lineage without distortions. This purity or essence of a lineage is held by genuine and realized masters who preserve, propagate, and transmit the authentic teachings and methods. This purity or essence encompasses the expression of individual realization (*men ngak* in Tibetan), the precious blessing (*jinlap* in Tibetan) and the oral instructions (*dam ngak* in Tibetan). This is why for Vajrayana practice, it is customary to find a teacher who is connected to a lineage.

Men Ngak

It is difficult to translate the term *"men ngak."* It refers to the qualities, or qualifications of a realized teacher or master. The teacher must possess accurate understanding of the teachings. He must have practiced the methods properly to become realized himself. This then qualifies him to share the methods and experiences with others. Moreover, the teacher is the one who connects the students to their inner potential that is Buddha-nature. It is by means of the teacher's *men ngak* that we are able to practice, to understand and to communicate with our inner potential through the practice. This is why a teacher is indispensable in Vajrayana practice. Three conditions must come together to enable us to practice in order to ultimately recognize Buddha-nature. We have to receive the expression of realization, the blessing, and the oral instructions from a qualified teacher. This is why the teacher must possess *men ngak* so that he can give us the explanations, instructions, and blessings enabling us to do the practice.

Jinlap

Again, there is no exact translation for the term, "blessing." Here is an example of how blessing works. Whenever we don't understand something in our practice, the blessing helps us to understand. Let's say we don't understand what mind is. It is not so easy to know what mind means. We hear words like mind, or Buddha-nature, but we can only guess at its meaning. We may hear the qualities of the awakened mind explained to us, but we feel we don't really understand the terms. The understanding will come when we engage in a practice such as the practice of Guru Yoga or Chenrezik. Each practice is communication. Normally, communication means communication in words. But in Vajrayana practices, the reciting of the practice texts, the visualization and the receiving of a *yidam's*[17] essence and qualities constitute communication. The qualities of the *yidam* entering our mind means that we connect to the *yidam's* realization, understanding of the mind, and Buddha-nature. It is blessing that renders this connection possible. On the surface, it may look as if it is a wish or a prayer. In actuality, we are already employing the Vajrayana methods. Through regular practice, the words and explanations will start to make sense to us. We have not created the answers ourselves obviously. It is the blessing that connects us to the understanding. It is very difficult to show this effect. By knowing that this kind of effect can take place, we will understand it as such when we experience it. Though this information is important, it does not mean that we can or should immediately use it. Instead, we try to see if it works for us. *The Songs of Milarepa*[18] contains many of these points, which are clearly presented and easy to understand. It is an excellent source of reference.

Dam Ngak

"Oral instructions" or *"dam ngak"* refers to the

---

[17] A *yidam* in the form of a meditation deity is an aspect of Buddhahood embodying certain enlightened qualities. In Vajrayana, a *yidam* practice is an expedient means to liberate the practitioner by connecting him to the enlightened qualities expressed by that particular *yidam*.

[18] See Garma C. Chang, *The Hundred Thousand Songs of Milarepa*: Boston, Shambala Publications, 1999.

clear and precise transmission of the words of the teachings. In the context of the relationship between a Dharma teacher and student, "oral instructions" points to a clear connection wherein the student has a feeling of genuine trust free of doubts and negativities. The disciple relies completely on the teacher to explain and instruct him on the meaning of the teachings and practices. We can look to the biographies of Marpa (1012-1097), Milarepa , and the Karma-pas, who are the lineage masters within the Kagyü tradition for examples of the oral instructions between teacher and student. Historical biographies of famous figures like Napoleon inform us of the time, place and descriptions of past events. But contained within the life-histories of the great masters like Saraha (1012-1097), Tilopa (988-1069), and Naropa (1016-1100) are treasuries of Dharma transmissions based on oral instructions.

In order for a certain result to happen, certain conditions and requirements must be present. To cure an illness, the appropriate medicine must be taken. *Dam ngak* works in a similar way. When we are lacking in understanding or when we need to know what to do, or we need an explanation or instruction, the oral instructions of the masters give us the answer. It is important for practitioners to know this so that when they read the biography of Milarepa, for instance, they will recognize and learn the relevant meanings. Otherwise, reading the biography as history would not be helpful at all. The clear transmission from teacher to disciple, or *dam ngak*, may be better illustrated by the following example of a story from *The Life and Teachings of Naropa*. Naropa was a great pandit[19] of Buddhism at the Nalanda University in India. Still, Naropa pined for higher teachings. This shows that learning is indeed limitless. Naropa felt the need to have a great instructor. When he first heard the name, Tilopa, he knew instantly that he must look for him. This was Naropa's own understanding, and therefore not applicable to everyone. But for Naropa, Tilopa was not so easy to find because he hid and disguised himself so that Naropa could not find him. It was for a very good reason – Tilopa wanted Naropa to go through a rigorous self-examination so as to reach the right understanding. Here is a passage from *The Life and Teachings of Naropa*:

On a narrow road, he (Naropa) met a stinking bitch crawling with vermin. He plugged his nose and jumped over the animal which then appeared in the sky in a rainbow-like halo and said:

"All living beings by nature are one's parents.
How will you find the Guru, if
Without developing compassion
On the Mahayana path
You seek in the wrong direction?
How will you find the Guru to accept you
When you look down on others?"

---

[19] A pandit is a scholar of the highest ranking.

After these words the bitch and the rocks disappeared and Naropa again found himself in a swoon on a sandy plateau[20].

When Naropa saw the wretched animal, he did not pay it any attention. He knew very well the concept of compassion yet in the face of the dog's suffering, he left it unattended. Preoccupied with finding Tilopa, he hurried away in pursuit of his own interest. From this incident, Naropa understood that he had not yet truly engaged in the enlightened attitude. Without this genuine motivation, he would not gain any realization. Naropa understood this point through *dam ngak.*

The oral instructions or *pith* (or pointing-out) transmissions all lead to the understanding of the essential meanings point by point. Their purpose is to clarify whatever it is that we don't understand so they are not exclusive to one tradition or lineage. They are important to you whether you are a researcher or a student of the Dharma, or a practitioner who is engaged in Vajrayana practices. Only then can you recognize the meaning when an opportunity arises. Oral instructions are essential in the transmission of the Mahamudra teaching and the like. Like Naropa, we have to be prepared or qualified to receive the transmission. Otherwise, even if Buddha were here, we would still not achieve any realization. Naropa immediately realized the lesson through *dam ngak*, not just once, but

[20] Guenther, *The Life and Teachings of Naropa*: New York, Oxford University Press, 1963, p. 30-31.

on twelve different occasions. The details are very precise and they are all recounted in his biography. This kind of biography is invaluable to us. The *dam ngak* teachings contained therein are vast and unlimited.

Whether or not we can achieve some result in our practice depends on our effort. When we work with the practice, we are developing our capacity to understand. No one can see this capacity in another. Everyone has some form of potential due to the preparations or accumulations done in previous lifetimes. Some of our past accumulations ripen in this lifetime. This explains why for some people, practice comes easily while it proves difficult for others. The Buddha taught us not to judge other people, not to judge situations as good or bad, right or wrong. We don't really know.

In the Vajrayana teachings, there are Tibetan terms such as *jinlap* and *men ngak* that are useful to know. There are no English words that fit their precise meanings. Though we don't fully understand them now, nevertheless, it is good to keep them in mind. We try to connect to their meaning so as to become properly directed. Through our own experience, we will be able to recognize the relevant meanings when they appear to us. We will be able to recognize and adjust our mistakes and move on. As well, we will be able to recognize misrepresentations of the teachings. This is how the knowledge of these terms will help us.

For example, the main meditation to achieve enlightenment is called Mahamudra. The term,

Mahamudra, is difficult to translate because there is no word for it. What it really means comes through one's experience by one's own practice and efforts. Moreover, it requires the transmission of the methods and knowledge from past masters who have already realized the results by the Mahamudra methods. By knowing this explanation about Mahamudra, we will carefully choose a qualified master. We will not go in search of a shortcut nor wait for something miraculous to happen to us. We know that to realize Mahamudra, we have to put in our own effort under the guidance of an authentic realized master.

APPROACH AND RESULTS OF VAJRAYANA PRACTICE

In Vajrayana, there are many practices such as Chenrezik, Green Tara, Dorje Sempa, and Amitabha. They are important regular practices with varying results or effects. Generally, the effects of each practice are twofold. First, each practice enables us to discover our own inner potential whereby we will realize our Buddha-nature. Second, each practice has special qualities that afford us temporary help specific to our current situation. For example, the practice of Tara can give us protection against fears or troubles. This is its special quality. Whenever we are in difficult times, and we don't know what to do, we practice Tara. Similarly, the practice of Dorje Sempa can help to clear up and purify our negativities. The Chenrezik practice is aimed at benefiting others through the development of the quality of *bodhicitta*. This will result in our helpfulness to others quite naturally. For each practice, the result is equally there regardless of whether we follow a short, or a long text.

We often ask for "blessing" but what is our understanding of it? The ultimate meaning of blessing is to enable us to connect to the special qualities inherent in the practices that we do. It is like sitting in a dark room and you want to let the sunlight in. But if you don't know how to open the curtains, the sunlight cannot shine through. When we understand the terms such as *dam ngak* or *jinlap*, we will know clearer as to what to expect from our practice. Otherwise, our expectations will not be quite right. Of course, some results are always there when we pray, or when we recite the mantras, but the main effect is our connecting to the qualities that the practices are supposed to develop. For example, the real meaning of the practice of Chenrezik is to become like Chenrezik and to act like him – being beneficial to others and free of ignorance. This is real not just information. For now, we may not have this wish to be Chenrezik. Individually, each of us may have different reasons in doing Buddhist practice. Regardless, we will gain some benefit from our efforts. But if we truly engender *bodhicitta*, then the result can be ever stronger and limitless.

This brings us to the efficacy of Vajrayana practice which depends very much on the individual. Everything is possible but not necessarily tangible. Much like the elementary particles discovered in High Energy Physics that we cannot see or touch, yet they are there in the connections of things. What is most essential and basic in Vajrayana practice is the connection. During the practice, it is not important how we feel or what we observe, rather, it is our understanding of being present in mind that matters. Of course having some experience is important but not having them is also important. It is a matter of concept. We are, for the moment, heavily engrossed in our concepts. Our expectations are likewise shaped. We are always waiting for a visible result. What is developed through the practice is a basic way of functioning, a basic quality in the practitioner that may or may not be available for use immediately. Some people mistakenly think that in Vajrayana practice, something powerful, miraculous, or magical would happen. Actually, it is not like that at all! The principal qualities of mind are naturally there and can be developed by any individual. Out of that, of course, many things are possible which have nothing to do with magic or trickery and they are not the aim of Vajrayana. But if our mind is caught up with these preoccupations, then we are in fact blocked from developing our potential. It is difficult to understand the details of how things work, but if we do the practice consistently, we will, very naturally, come to some understanding of its meaning. We always keep in mind the essence of the practice. For example, when we do the Chenrezik practice, we sit, we recite, and we meditate. But afterwards, away from the practice, we try to keep the same altruistic attitude and presence of mind in whatever we do. This is what it means to keep the essence of the practice. We take the example of the candlelight and the sunlight. A candle offers a little light in darkness, but the sun really illuminates. The sun has much greater capacity than a candle. Our capacity at the moment is like that of the candle. It offers some light. Through the practice, we combine our light with the sun's rays to become ever stronger. It is important to practice regularly so that our own capacity could grow and strengthen steadily. If we can do it, then naturally, we will become clearer and our actions increasingly beneficial to others. Our positive qualities will develop. This will happen naturally much like how the grass grows - we cannot see the grass actually growing, but rest assured, it is.

EMPOWERMENT [21]

Before we do a Vajrayana practice such as Dorje Sempa, it is customary to receive an initiation from a qualified teacher. All Vajrayana practices appear to have certain rituals, which are of relative importance. Each component of the ritual has a very precise meaning. They are, however, not important in the absolute sense. An example to illustrate this point is the need for heating and plumbing in our home. These are important amenities yet they are not crucial to our survival. Similarly, the rituals are there to help us but beyond that, they have no absolute importance.

---

[21] Also called initiation; it is *wang* in Tibetan or *abhisheka* in Sanskrit.

There are in general three aspects to an initiation. The first is the instructions on the practice (*tri* in Tibetan). Next is a reading transmission of the practice (*lung* in Tibetan). The third is the empowerment itself (*wang* in Tibetan) which enables the initiate to do the practice. During any initiation, what is important is to be continuously present. This means to try to have our attention on what is taking place. We are holding the meaning of the initiation throughout, from the time leading up to the conferring of the initiation, the actual initiation, and its conclusion. Our wish to be initiated will then be fulfilled and our mind will be integrated with the essence of the practice.

In Tibetan, *kyerim* means to create, and *dzokrim* means to integrate or to unite with what has been created. These are the two stages of an initiation. To create does not mean to make something solid in form. The pure *yidam* and his environment visualized during *kyerim* is the preparation performed by the qualified master. Then, during the stage of *dzokrim* we are connected to the purity of the *yidam* at our individual potential. When we say the connection is through our body, speech, and mind, it is symbolic but not artificial. It is symbolic of the connection we have made at our current level so that we will be able to develop and purify, to the fullest extent, our own potential. It is important to have this proper understanding when we choose to receive an initiation. During the initiation, our attitude should be directed to engendering the enlightened attitude. Our single most earnest concern is for the well being of others so we take on the practice to better ourselves in order that we may become more beneficial and helpful to others. Without this crucial motivation, we may receive some small blessings, but we have missed the point of the Buddha's teachings. When we are correctly oriented in enlightened attitude, we will improve little by little until we reach true understanding. To improve means to obtain further understanding through the practice. Take for example our idea of mind. We don't really have an understanding of what it is, or what it means exactly. We can only guess at its meaning. Gradually, by doing the practice, we will come to discover what mind is.

DEVELOP NATURALLY THE INNER CONDITIONS

A person's fundamental capacity varies between individuals but it can be developed gradually through practice. The progress cannot be forced. It has to develop spontaneously. Spontaneity depends on whether we see the meaning of the teachings. When we get the point, spontaneity is right there. It is like when you are sick and the doctor tells you to eat this and not that. But sometimes, you yourself know precisely which foods to avoid. You really understand your own situation. You know spontaneously by yourself. It is very simple when we get the exact meaning. When we think of enlightenment, we may feel that it is so far away or that it is going to take a long time. But sometimes, it is really not that impossible when all the conditions are right. We should carry on with the practice without analyzing it too much.

As explained earlier, due to the blessings of the transmission lineage, some result is inevitably there. They are the inner conditions that will enhance our receptiveness to the teachings thereby effectively connecting us to their essence. These inner conditions are confidence and devotion, authentic faith and the right connection.

Mögü

The first condition is *"mögü"* in Tibetan; again it is a very difficult notion to translate. It is an inner condition that we need when we receive the teachings, which is our complete trust and respect for the enlightened qualities. Its effect upon us is our deep appreciation and recognition of the importance of the enlightened qualities. The result is a deep wish to follow the path of practice and a strong conviction that we can do it. *Mögü* gives us the proper perspective enabling us to go deeper into the meaning without getting stuck in our development. For example, our confidence and devotion towards the Buddha, Dharma, and Sangha are very important while we are on the path of practice and in this context, we can interpret *mögü* as devotion and confidence. In the biography of Milarepa, his devotion and confidence were so evident and powerful that they catapulted him to full enlightenment in one lifetime. Milarepa's perseverance rooted in his deep devotion to Marpa never faltered. *Mögü* was thus the main cause for Milarepa's realization.

Depa

The second inner condition, similar to *mögü*, is *depa* which means faith. But it is not blind faith. It requires real understanding in what we are doing so we have conviction. The basis of our faith is more than just because someone told us we should, or we are so impressed that we want to follow. When we have done the proper study and research, we arrive at an understanding that enables us to really focus and stay committed, that is *depa*.

Damtsik

The third condition is *damtsik*. *Damtsik* is *samaya* in Sanskrit, it means to have the right connection to the essence of our own mind. It means that when we act properly, good results are inevitable. When we make mistakes, our path will be blocked. How we judge and act are both directly related to our own mind so we always want to be careful.

Our thoughts, inner attitudes and conditions of mind have far greater reach and effect than our actions. But normally, we control our actions rather than our minds. When we dislike someone, we don't want to show it. We are afraid that it will spoil our image of being nice. But inside, we are feeling our dislike for the contact. We try to be nice because we may not want to break up the friendship. Unconsciously, we

go on like this. We need to understand our own
mind rather than just trying to control our actions. Sometimes, we think, *"I don't want to
help;"* or *"I don't like it;"* or *"I don't want to
give in anymore."* These thoughts are not the
right connections so they can block us. This we
should know and understand very clearly. Because *damtsik* is a realization of mind that is
linked to our understanding. This is why in the
Vajrayana, pure vision is emphasized which is
in itself a state of mind. It is seeing perfectly
without veils and distortions. It is not something
artificial that someone told us about. It comes
from our own basic nature. It is part of our consciousness. If we want to realize pure vision,
then we need to receive teachings, learn to see
clearly, and meditate. We have to develop ourselves, our actions are not all that important in
and of themselves. The problems are the blockages in our minds that influence our actions. We
cannot block them out to avoid damages. We
have to understand how they are actually related to us, to our mind.

These three conditions, *mögü, depa,* and
damtsik are qualities that have to be developed.
Having been introduced to them, we need to
carefully consider their deeper meaning. What
do they really mean to us, individually? We
don't gloss over them with English terms such
as confidence, faith, devotion, etc., and think
that we understand already. For example, we all
know what faith means. But what does faith really mean in you? What does confidence mean
when you have it or when you don't? You have

to inspect your own conditions to find out for yourself. Try to connect more to the deeper meaning. Our original associations with these terms will change over with experience and time.

To develop our understanding is much like getting a suntan. It won't work if we go into the sun fully clothed wearing a hat. Even after a long while, we will not tan, we may feel warmer perhaps. Uncovering ourselves is a condition that has to happen first, and then our exposed skin will naturally tan. Similarly, our understanding will also come about naturally when we embrace *mögü*, *depa* and *damtsik*. They are the main conditions that facilitate a deeper understanding of our own mind. The depth of knowledge is unlimited so we continuously work with our inner understanding through our practice, while listening to the teachings, or during the normal course of the day. In this way, our understanding will mature until it is fully integrated into our way of thinking. We often hear the descriptive, "inseparable". It means inseparable from our mind. It is then our mind. Nothing is created. It is important that we put in the effort. By gradually clearing up the questions and doubts, we will develop a personal experience that is genuinely mind.

Authentic Master and Ordinary Lama

The Buddha elucidated the truth of liberation from the problems of *samsara*. Those who followed and applied his teachings, and accomplished the results are referred to as realized masters. In fact, many texts were written and are still being written by these masters. They are the extraordinary spiritual friends who can show us how to follow the Dharma path of liberation. The different categories of spiritual friends are explained in Gampopa's *The Jewel Ornament of Liberation*. Authentic or realized masters are considered extraordinary teachers because they have realized the results of the path. They are bodhisattvas working for sentient beings in accordance with the Dharma.

AUTHENTIC MASTER

An authentic master should be connected to a Buddhist lineage. This means that by following such a master we are also connected to the lineage. As well we are connected to all the past masters like a chain linked all the way back to the Buddha. This is very important because in this way we can avoid mistakes or misuse of the teachings.

The realized lineage holders designed effective practices to help the practitioners. These methods have been passed down to us through the generations of lineage masters. There are also practice texts and notes preserved to this day available to us. Even today, realized lineage masters are revising some practices not because they have flaws but to make them more suitable for us in our modern conditions. These in turn will also be passed down to the future generations. It is not so easy to modify the practices because the meaning can be unknowingly altered. This is why only authentic lineage holders are qualified to make the revisions. We in turn follow the practices properly without any extraneous additions or adjustments to keep the methods and meanings intact.

In some practices we recite the names of the lineage holders to remember them in order to connect with them. The connection enhances our potential for understanding. From the early teachers like Marpa, to Milarepa, to Gampopa, to the First Karmapa and all the way to the present time, we can now connect to them all through our teacher. This may be difficult for us to appreciate because we don't yet understand. Nevertheless, we can connect to our teacher by our devotion, faith, and confidence because he is here. Gendun Rinpoche[22] was one example of an authentic master.

Throughout the ages, practitioners who studied and practiced successfully became authentic masters. Some of them started at a young age while others started late. Gampopa started when he was forty-five years old and still succeeded in bringing his practice to fruition. Gampopa lived a house-holder's life until he met the great master, Milarepa, and practiced under his guidance. It is therefore possible for us to do the same.

The qualities of an authentic master can manifest through many different activities. But the principal quality is that his mind is completely pure. It means that if we try to find even one fault in him, we will not find it. Fault in this context means a mistake in judgment. It was difficult to find fault with Gendun Rinpoche, as his mind was very pure. On a relative level, people might have thought his English was not very good neither was his French, so communication with him was difficult. But people who looked at his way of thinking, his actions, and his way of understanding sensed his purity. This purity can move you and raise your devotion, confidence, etc. Following someone without seeing the perfect qualities is like blind faith or fanaticism.

---

[22] A Tibetan master (1918-1987) who devoted his life to meditative practice especially in solitary retreats. In 1975, the 16th Karmapa sent him to France to teach, to give Westerners access to authentic teachings of the Buddha. He founded many retreat centers and a monastic hermitage called Dhagpo Kundreul Ling.

Because our tendencies and conditions of mind are strong, it is difficult for us to change. For this reason, we rely on a master as our spiritual role model. Very often, we find that when we want to change, we can't. Even in everyday life when we know a better way to do something, we often forego it because we are reluctant to change. The main point of all teachings is to help us change. A realized teacher who is authentic in practice, attitude, and action serves as our model. Authentic does not refer to the physical or outer form of behavior. In general, people in our society are impressed by exterior appearances. Someone dressed in a special robe talking very nicely can impress us. But what of his inner qualities? A qualified teacher's attitudes and motivations should be completely in line with the Dharma and connected to the qualities of Buddha-nature which are inevitably perfect.

His Holiness the late 16th Gyalwa Karmapa[23] always cautioned his disciples to be aware of our intentions and attitudes. He told us to check for self-grasping – a feeling that we are very important. Even when it is not strongly evident in us, we are somehow always looking after our own interests. We do everything for ourselves grasping ever more tightly and we quickly lose sight of our goal. Karma, in the meantime, is fully active. While causes are continuing to be created, the effects will surely ripen one day. The pursuit after name, fame, riches, intelligence, political influence and

---

[23] Rangjung Rikpé Dorjé (1924-1981).

so on, has its source in clinging to the self as all-important. Naturally, looking after ourselves to a large degree is normal and basic but living as independent and responsible individuals is also important. We can live without self-importance, an attachment which leads only to problems and suffering. Even our wish to become like the Buddha, or to be free from suffering, if it is motivated by self-grasping, then all the problems will continue for us. We will never understand these problems. We may be very nice people, but if we don't see our problems, that in-itself is a problem. When His Holiness Karmapa first explained this, it was not so easy to really see his point. But over time, we came to appreciate the significance of his advice. He used to ask us to forget about ourselves, and to act more for others. He said that our lives would then be very useful, and we would be happy, which was what we all wanted. This lesson from the Karmapa is exactly what the central theme of the teachings of the Buddha is: *samsara* is suffering, and *bodhicitta* will bring happiness to us and others. This runs contrary to the common worldly view of looking after "me" first lest others take "my" happiness away.

The inner attitude of the authentic teacher underlies everything he is and does. He acts solely for the benefit of others even in the little things he does. His inner motivation is not on public display. If someone is showing off how caring he is, then he is not genuine. We should try to check the teacher because he is someone in whom we will rely. We will model after him.

As well, through him who carries the transmission of the lineage, we will follow the links, one to one, all the way to the Buddha.

Take the example of Gendun Rinpoche. He did not speak Western languages. He did not read the newspaper. He did not listen to the radio. He seemed isolated. But ask him a question, he would immediately give a very clear answer. You might have been thinking incessantly about a problem making it very complicated and confusing to you. But Gendun Rinpoche could set you straight in an instant. *"Ah, so it is like this..."* so you might think afterwards. It is the same with a car mechanic. He knows how to repair a car because he is clear about its parts and functions.

ORDINARY LAMA

How we relate to the authentic master is dependent on our level of understanding and our knowledge of the mind. As explained before, our store of merits determines to a large degree how receptive we are. For people who don't have the predisposition to connect readily, Gampopa emphasized the importance of an ordinary lama. He is someone who can start you off learning about the Dharma until you can relate to an authentic master in a meaningful way. Otherwise, due to the mental veils in the minds of sentient beings, we may not recognize an authentic master right before us.

Most people want to find the best or highest teacher. The trouble is our judgment is somewhat constricted by our view. This narrowing can adversely affect our relationship with an authentic master, so there is not a good fit. This is why in *The Jewel Ornament of Liberation*, Gampopa stressed that ordinary teachers are very important to us. They introduce us to the path of Dharma. They instruct us and give us explanations on the Dharma. They prepare us, and help us to develop. Otherwise, we will continue in our habitual ways unwilling to change for the better. It is difficult for people to change their minds. An example, we know what paper is. If someone tries to tell us otherwise, we will not believe him. The belief or recognition comes from within and so must the change. Ordinary lamas can help us get the meaning so we know what to look for and how to make adjustments. They enable us to break free of preconceptions and habitual thinking.

We can relate to an "ordinary" lama on a personal level. Nevertheless, whether a lama is ordinary or extraordinary, for him to qualify as a spiritual friend, he must possess certain conditions, characteristics, and knowledge. *"La"* in Tibetan means higher in knowledge than us. *"Ma"* is someone who takes care of us. "Lama" then points to a spiritual guide who can explain to us the path and achievement of Buddhahood.

A Buddhist teacher must possess a really compassionate mind, which is an indispensable quality. He volunteers his service to helping others. His disposition is one of tireless patience, and he is always careful in his words aiming to benefit others. His compassion will naturally multiply as he performs his activities grounded in the enlightened attitude. We should not expect him to be like the great realized bodhisattvas, but rather as someone who truly embraces the enlightened attitude. Gampopa described a "common" or "ordinary" lama as not being perfect, the same as we are. We don't expect the lama to be perfect. If we do, it will create problems. The ordinary lama is special because he engenders *bodhicitta*. His guidance should be pure without self-interest, or wanting to be special. Without this sincere commitment, even if the person can explain the terms and meanings of the teachings to us, he may at the same time influence us through his tendencies thus misleading us towards the wrong direction. So we have to be careful and follow a teacher who has the proper attitude of *bodhicitta*. Of course, we cannot really see someone's motivation. We can, however, recognize people who think themselves very important. To embrace *bodhicitta* does not mean to talk nicely, and to put on a smile. *Bodhicitta* points to a mind that is very clear, very pure. It may be found in someone who appears rough in his mannerisms, but underneath the exterior shell, there is no grasping, no hatred, or ill intention.

The ordinary lama must know the teachings. He is learned and familiar with the different subjects of Buddhist teachings. He studies, practices, and applies the teachings in his daily life. By engaging himself in practice in this way, he receives the blessings of the realized masters. This is a very natural process. It is through the practice that he is connected to an extraordinary master, or a *yidam*, who is a form of bodhisattva in Vajrayana practice. Therefore, any spiritual guide must combine both practice and learning together.

We have to understand that we will see faults in the ordinary lama. The mistakes we see in others often are our own concepts. We are always judgmental and critical, it is difficult to find someone perfect. Criticism appears when we are obscured by our own knowledge and ideas, so much so that when a new, or different idea comes into our view, we reject it right away. There is no room to accommodate anything or anyone different from us. This means that we are blocking ourselves. We keep looking but we cannot find that perfect one. In the meantime, we achieve nothing.

Emotions can be changed and turned into both "path" and "result". They can lead us to mind's nature so they are like a path; and they can turn into a realization of mind which is a result. Fundamental to all Dharma teachings is the goal to understand the natural functioning of mind. Emotions can open the door into an inner understanding of ourselves. Take any emotion, and try to understand it more clearly by observing it and then reflecting on it. Practice like this and try to learn from it. When we find ourselves pre-occupied with judging others, we remind ourselves that they are human beings, too, like us. This, in turn, will actually help us understand ourselves by developing a pure mind. Pure mind does not mean to just think purely of someone, which does not make sense. A pure mind recognizes the basic conditions of being human. These include, ignorance, afflicting emotions, prejudices, self-projections, and so on. We have them all because we are human. Whether we are dealing with the lama or with people in general, it is very beneficial to be aware of our mental veils caused by our emotions and biases.

Just as we keep an open mind about the lama, we also try to be aware of our prejudices and concepts in our dealings with people. We will come to understand even more clearly the obscurations based in our emotions, habitual tendencies, and pre-conceptions. We again apply this knowledge during our interactions with others. Otherwise, the teachings remain mere words to us. It is very easy to work with our children, family, and friends. These relationships reveal many conditions about us. When we see more clearly our own inner conditions, again try to reflect more deeply. This is the process by which we can improve. The teachings always emphasize the importance of ethical conduct. Just as we understand to avoid negative friends, it makes sense then that we want to be a positive friend to others. We continue to practice, introspect, and apply our understanding in daily life. In this way, our knowledge of how we function will grow. This is really a fundamental purpose of our relationship with the lama.

An ordinary lama is someone who has a *bodhicitta* mind. This means that he has a proper attitude, and he abides by proper ethic. He has achieved some practices, and he can teach. When we first set out to learn about the Dharma, an ordinary teacher is important because it is easier to relate to him. He is a spiritual friend more advanced than us in his grasp of the Dharma. The word, "spiritual", is used as opposed to worldly because he gives us information about the authentic teachings of the Buddha and of the great masters. Therefore, we need to have a certain degree of confidence and respect towards him as our teacher. We follow his instructions and apply them in practice. We are sure to achieve some results through our efforts. This means that we will accumulate merit which in turn will bring about favorable conditions where we will encounter the bodhisattvas, or the extraordinary masters in a meaningful way. When we do, we won't waste such good opportunities. More importantly, an ordinary lama serves us well by preparing us to connect to realized masters.

There are different ways of relating to the lama. The basic one is where the student receives instructions from the teacher and applies them in practice. Provided we have the proper understanding as explained already, it is not difficult to relate to a teacher. Otherwise, we may get stuck and unable to fully benefit from the relationship. Our concepts and opinions often block us from seeing things differently. For example, when we hear the word, "love", each of us has pre-conceived ideas about it. The one term connotes different kinds of love. As well, each of us experiences the meaning differently.

Most of us are aware of these differences and so we are careful in our interpretations and communications. Likewise, we need to keep an open mind when we relate to the lama.

When we meet an authentic teacher and receive teachings from him, we may feel somewhat connected, but at the same time, we may also pull back a little thinking, *"I can't think of the lama as a buddha. I can't think that he's completely pure."* These doubts can arise in the mind. It is therefore helpful to study the historical lama-disciple relationships. By studying how Milarepa related to his teacher, Marpa, we can be clearer about the qualities of a master. At the same time, we learn how the masters in the past trained when they were themselves disciples. Again on this subject, *The Jewel Ornament of Liberation* by Gampopa, is an excellent reference. It gives a detailed description of the qualifications of a master. It explains the different levels of teachers, from the ordinary lama as a teacher of Dharma to the bodhisattva or extraordinary spiritual friend who has attained some level of realization. We can therefore study carefully the classifications and explanations by Gampopa and reach a better understanding.

On the Part of the Disciple

MERITS

The accumulation of merit is very important for our Dharma practice. We want to first understand properly the precise meaning of "merit" in this context. Merit is commonly understood to be the cause of good fortune in life as in having success in what we do, or to be in good circumstances. This is not the kind of merit accumulation we need for our practice. To illustrate the meaning of merit here, take this example of pouring water onto a piece of paper. The water simply flows off the paper. Paper does not have the capacity to hold water. Similarly, without merit, mind does not have the capacity to comprehend clearly. So we say that the merit we want to accumulate is for mind to have the capacity to understand correctly the meaning of the Dharma.

Even when we agree with the teachings, it does not mean we get the meaning. To get the meaning, we need to have an accumulation of merit. Merit varies widely between individuals. Gampopa said that some people can get the meaning right away while others cannot due to a difference in their merits. We cannot judge whether or not someone has merit. People whose minds are clear or who can easily understand the Dharma have been accumulating merit since their past lives. Others who have not accumulated merit can still develop the ability to understand. It will take them longer. This shows how important merit or *sonam* (Tibetan) is. It directly impacts our ability to understand clearly.

The Jewel Ornament of Liberation explains that the inner potential or capacity of a disciple is dependent entirely on merit – a disciple's "basic karma." Our capacity to understand is thus based on our own merit. How we view things is directly linked to our merit. We should take the time to consider the significance of merit.

On the surface, to relate to the lama or teacher sounds easy enough especially when things are going well. However, when doubts and contradictions arise, we are at a loss as to how to deal. We really struggle then to gain more clarity. But we can only have a certain degree of understanding governed by our potential. Therefore, we should not try to understand as much as someone else can, for instance. Rather, we work on developing our inner potential. We can do this under the guidance of our teacher. Having obtained the right instructions, we can begin to apply the methods. In this way, we will improve our understanding steadily without hurry or pressure. Even when we start to improve, it is nothing special either. We continue to relate to the teacher in the only way we know how - based on our inner understanding. There is no other way.

At the moment, our mind is blocked so we cannot see our true nature and that of our world. While our mind is in ignorance, we are caught up in an illusion of existence. The Madhyamaka view (the highest Buddhist philosophical view) elucidates in great detail this hindrance that is in our mind now – about ignorance, the illusions, and how to liberate from them. Even when we have the explanations, we still cannot have a precise idea about these conditions. Illusion is a very profound concept. Our understanding of it has to be very precise so as to get its full meaning. The Madhyamaka view is founded on rigorous analysis and complex logical deduction. This view coupled with actual meditation experience will yield the ultimate clarity by which we can become enlightened, liberated from ignorance.

Needless to say, the Madhyamaka view is not easy to grasp. The words sound straightforward enough but great merit is required. Again, people associate merit as having a good life, an easy life wherein things are going relatively well. Sometimes we think, *"I have a lot of problems, or I'm not really successful, this must mean that I've no merit."* This is not necessarily the case. Look up the biographies of the great *siddhas*. A *siddha* is someone with a deep realization of mind. We will find that the *siddhas* were very often clever practitioners but they were unsuccessful in life in the ordinary sense. Their success came only after practicing the Dharma until they were realized. In this context, merit actually can manifest as obstacles in everyday life. These may be in the form of frustrations, or unsuccessful endeavors that turn someone towards Dharma practice eventually leading to the ultimate achievement of awakened mind. This is why we don't need to get down on ourselves thinking, *"I am not so happy. I cannot find the meaning of life. So many things did not work out for me so I must have very bad karma!"* We should not think like that. Of course, ordinary merit can mean things go well for us and life is good. The transitory gains in everyday life are not important. What is important are the right circumstances and the merit to practice the Dharma. And Gampopa stated very clearly that the means to accumulate such merit is entirely dependent on the spiritual friend.

POSITIVE RESULTS BORN OF DIFFICULTIES

From the biography of Milarepa, it is evident that were it not for the mistreatments he suffered during childhood, Milarepa would not have achieved enlightenment. All the problems that confronted him made him look for a way out which ultimately led him to his teacher, Marpa. His problems did not end after meeting Marpa. As a teacher, Marpa was unrelenting in creating challenges and demands on Milarepa to enable him to attain real understanding. Some people may misconstrue Marpa's treatment as torture when in actual fact, the trials and tribulations were effective means to open Milarepa's mind and brought his inner understanding to a full realization of mind that is enlightenment.

Similarly, we should look upon our own conditions and experiences, good or bad, to use them to learn more about how our mind functions. We open ourselves to the choices in life ever mindful of what really matters. In general, we are somewhat blocked or close-minded, expecting things to be a certain way. At times, we are blocked by our emotions, which are our own basic conditions. Try to see that things don't necessarily work just one way. Try to be more open to the different possibilities that can work just as well, if not better. Our perspective and understanding will change. Sometimes, we may feel that we also need to undergo the same ordeals as Milarepa did to purify ourselves and to develop the merit. Again, the point is that there are different ways for different people, not only one way. Milarepa's disciple, Rechungpa (1083-1161), and many past masters did not have to go through grueling challenges. Actually, what limits our mind is our view that there is only one way. Something worked for others and we jump to the conclusion that it has to be that way for us, too, and no other way.

However, an essential point in how we relate to the teacher or lama to arrive at a greater understanding of ourselves is to be very open. This means we need space in our own mind. It is hard to understand this space because we are blocked by our "concrete" ideas. There is no room for inspection. Space means "chance to look deeper" so we can better understand. We can again draw on Naropa's search for Tilopa to get some idea. Tilopa had emanated in the guise of a dog with a worm-infested wound. Naropa saw the dog's suffering, but he failed to help the dog because he was too "blocked" by his desire to find Tilopa. At that point, Tilopa revealed himself to Naropa saying, "If you have no compassion, then the lama is useless to you." In this way, Tilopa made Naropa look deeper within to understand himself. We are often very mechanical in our thinking and behavior. We think that if we find the teacher, receive teachings and do the practice, then we will become realized. In a way, it is true but if we don't make good use of the circumstances that come our way, we will not get the results.

The meaning of Tilopa's lesson to Naropa is this: without true compassion towards sentient beings, then the lama is not important or serves no purpose. Tilopa transmitted this exact meaning to Naropa who really needed this lesson. Naropa thought he knew everything being one of the foremost scholars of his time. But Naropa still felt an inner drive to learn more, and thus set out to look for a master. Tilopa was successful in showing Naropa the essential points by twelve separate trials. Point by point, Naropa got all the meanings. Our path may not be exactly like Naropa's, but we should gain some understanding from this example.

Another lesson can be learned from this same example of Tilopa's appearing as a dog. We may think the appearance impossible so we call it a miracle. Here is again another example of our blockage. We can't do it, we don't understand it, so it must be a miracle! If we remain open, we will understand that when the mind is free, anything can happen from mind. This is beyond our comprehension now because we are stuck in our illusions. There are actually many different processes of mind. There are precise practices and explanations that can guide us towards more understanding. We will also come to know them through our practice. In the meantime, we settle for just being aware that mind has many more capabilities than what we are accustomed to.

Mind's nature is very profound and complex, and so in this respect, we say that it is difficult to realize. But again, the term "difficult" is only a relative concept. By looking to the past masters, how they practiced, and how they connected to their spiritual teachers, we can begin to understand. Without going into great lengths, it suffices to acknowledge that the relationship with the lama rests very much on the inner motivation, attitude and comprehension on the part of the disciple. This does not mean to be heavy-minded, thinking that you have to be like this or that, or a particular way. Again, it means that you should listen carefully, reflect carefully, and the understanding will come naturally. This is really not so difficult to do. However, if we try to be rigid in a certain way, then we will have problems. We cannot change overnight even if we put one hundred percent effort into it. By doing the practice, without any pressure, we will understand. The change in us will happen naturally. The method always consists of two steps: first, we understand, or we get the right idea, and then we put our understanding to practice. Both steps are reliant on our inner resolve and on our mind. This is a very important point. It prevents us from following blindly without understanding, which is blind faith. We follow our own understanding so we have to be very clear.

AN AUTHENTIC RELATIONSHIP

Again, the relationship between master and disciple depends on how the latter thinks, understands, and acts. There is no strict code of do's and don'ts. Our functioning is quite spontaneous. We can get some idea of how this works by looking at how we deal with small things in everyday life. We are creatures of habit. Those mental habits seem mixed in together with our preconceptions and ideas, the endless distractions, and all kinds of grasping. The habits are naturally there, try as we may, we cannot extract them, it is as if they are glued down. Just as our habits have grown natural to us over time, to change them also has to happen naturally in time.

There is a saying, "A good disciple always follows the perfect master." It means the disciple follows the example set by his teacher. He makes changes using his teacher as his role model. In the past in Tibet, the great masters were once disciples themselves who followed their teachers. A good disciple is not a copycat who follows superficially. He is not a robot which follows mechanically. He is not rigid following out of obligation without thinking. Like his teacher, a good disciple abides in the Dharma as a living experience. This points directly to a basic attitude, thinking and behavior perfectly in sync with the Dharma as demonstrated by the teacher. It is this basic core that the disciple follows and applies day in day out such that it becomes his nature. From this core, the student's ideas, attitudes, and actions will flow naturally, and perfectly. When that happens, the student has integrated the ways of the master into habits of mind. This is how great disciples became perfect masters themselves.

Many teenagers smoke to fit in. When the smoking becomes an addiction, it is difficult to break. Just as we can take on bad habits through the influence of our friends, we can surely take on good habits through our relationship with our spiritual teacher. A perfect relationship is one where all the qualities of the master enter the disciple. There are many past examples of this in Tibet. Some people think Tibetans are perfect. This is not true. They are the same as other peoples of the world. Perfection can only come to those who follow a perfect teacher. Of course, this is easier said than done. The disciple has to really go through all the practices properly before the results will appear naturally.

Therefore, we must earnestly relate to an authentic master. The relationship is neither ordinary nor exciting. We don't create any hype around it. Often, we encounter certain terms or ideas which excite us. Intrigued, we experiment with them by trying to feel or behave in a very superficial way. This is common in most people. However, when we practice the Dharma, Gampopa advised us to be very relaxed and stable. Our relationship with the master is no different. Here again, the goal is for us to become clear so we can help others. At the conclusion of some practices, we recite words which mean we become inseparable from the lama. This refers to achieving a specific state of mind. The emphasis here is "to achieve" not just "to try". Somehow, the word "try" connotes a habitual way of following which is not what we want here. Here we actually accomplish being one with the lama.

In *The Jewel Ornament of Liberation*, Gampopa explained the cause and results of *samsara*, and the cause and results of nirvana. By studying and understanding these connections, we will recognize what to do, and the right direction. Naturally we exert the right effort. Because we recognize the various factors that will bring about positive or negative results, we can relax. Relax does not mean to just sit and be quiet. We relax the mind from our excitement and pursuits. As a result, we become more stable. When we are not aware of our conditions, they sway us so we lose our balance. The same applies to the relationship with the lama, try to relax and steadily gain more insight. If we are full of wonderment, this creates tension which will block us even though there are junctures where the feeling of excitement is understandable. As the deeper meaning of the relationship become more apparent, we will calm down and stabilize. The stability will then develop on its own naturally.

The authentic master has realized the ultimate truth by himself. The Guru Yoga is a quick method to reach this same realization. Quick does not mean fast as in running. Rather, it signifies an efficacious method that enables us to connect to the master such that we too can accomplish the enlightened qualities. The Tibetan term for this method is *lamé neljor*. *"nel"* means part of us, and *"jor"* means to reach the result. Take again the example of getting a suntan, to get a tan, we have to be in the sun – that is *nel* or our participation which should not be forced. When our skin tans, we have result – that is *jor*. To tan, we simply wait in the sun. There is no pressure to do anything. It does not call for any effort on our part, strong or weak. We tan by the sheer nature of the sun. Our involvement is to be in the sun to absorb the sunrays. Similarly, *neljor* means we open up to our Buddha-nature. We are in the presence of all the positive qualities, and we will spontaneously receive the blessings. The realized bodhisattvas have the capacity to help us. The result is we understand our own mind. We may think we already understand ourselves. We know we have a mind. We know we have a name. We think we know who we are, but we don't really know precisely.

On a relative level, people practice Guru Yoga because they accept and believe what the teachings say. On an ultimate level, the relationship is one of inseparability, where the disciple becomes one with the qualities of the master. This has to be spontaneous. If you try to do it, it does not work. But if you just go along with it, it works. Still there are some very important points to understand, which are quite delicate and can easily be misconstrued.

In Guru Yoga we supplicate the master as the precious Buddha and as three enlightened aspects of Buddhahood in a four-line prayer. We also recite another request-prayer three times or more as follows:

"Precious master, I pray to you.
Grant your blessing so that my mind can let go of clinging to a self.
Grant your blessing so that I have contentment [24].
Grant your blessing so that thoughts that do not accord with the Dharma do not arise in me.
Grant your blessing so that I realize the unborn nature of mind.
Grant your blessing so that illusion dissolves by itself.
Grant your blessing so that manifestation actualizes as the body of truth."

The essence of this prayer is to request the master's blessing so that we may become realized. This prayer shows all the essential points exactly in the words we recite. The Guru Yoga

---

[24] It means we no longer have attachments.

thus opens us to accumulate the necessary merit crucial to a clear understanding of the meaning of those points. A similar effect is achieved by the practice of offering feast[25]. The rite is usually linked with a Guru Yoga practice. We offer an elaborate feast to the same master we supplicate in the Guru Yoga. For example, after we perform the Guru Yoga of Milarepa, we offer a feast to him. We need merit to appreciate the real significance behind the elaborate rite which may confuse some people. It is actually much more than just cultural tradition, ritual, or prayer. Its aim is again for us to gain clarity, to enhance our capacity to understand which is directly linked to merit.

In daily life, we have confidence in many things and people. But the confidence in the master is different. We may trust a car in good condition to cover a great distance without problems. We have confidence in good friends upon whom we can rely. These types of confidence afford us certain advantages and positive feelings in daily life. But the master offers us genuine benefit. Just like the sun whose rays tan our skin, the master's mind influences our mind to become clearer. The result is a real understanding of what it means to have *mögü*, *depa*, or *damtsik*. These inner qualities afford us pure vision and clarity of mind. We will therefore gain authentic knowledge, which is indeed a genuine benefit. In particular, we will come to appreciate the qualities of the master.

[25] *Ganachakra* in Sanskrit or *tsok* in Tibetan. It is a ritual and a specific practice of Vajrayana Buddhism.

In the presence of a highly realized master, if we are unclear, we will not see properly. The Buddha had a cousin who was very learned but lacked real understanding of the knowledge he had amassed. As a result, the cousin could not relate properly to the Buddha whom he criticized and challenged. Similarly, though we have received the teachings, it is up to us to really become clear about their meaning. We have to work with the teachings through careful examination and introspection. We have to do the practice and apply the methods (meditation, the practice of Guru Yoga, for example.) They serve only one purpose – to clear the mind of its veils. The results only and always come through as our own insights.

There is a prayer where we acknowledge that we are used to our way of seeing and thinking for many lifetimes now. We pray that the master will continue to be with us life after life until enlightenment. Of course, we pray that we could reach enlightenment but this is a long-term goal. Most of us are impatient. We want results immediately, or we lose interest. We like to work on things where we can get quick results. We are like this in everything we do. But when we follow the Dharma and study under a master, our commitment continues and ends only when we are enlightened. As well, we want to continue in a good way meaning to continue in a perfect life. This perfect life means a life connected to the authentic master without ever disconnected from the benefit of the Dharma. Life after life until enlightenment, we want to stay connected with the master. Through this connection, we will come to know all the knowledge of the Dharma. This fruition is explained in detail in the last chapter of Gampopa's book.

We are often told to relax in the practice. It does not really mean to relax in the ordinary sense. It does not mean to just sit and wait. Relax means not to put so much pressure on wanting or expecting a result. Knowing that enlightenment is a long-term goal, we learn to relax, and take our time to really see deeper and deeper into the innate functioning of mind. This insight functioning requires a certain degree of freedom from the influences of ignorance and confusion. It does not depend on age, worldly knowledge, or how clever we are. It is possible for each of us to know our basic nature. What matters is our inner preparation. Faith and devotion actually come natural to us. However, we have to prepare because our mind is at the moment veiled by our habitual tendencies, emotional afflictions, and obscurations of pre-conceptions. These negative conditions rooted in ignorance constitute a vast subject of Dharma study, not so easy to fathom in our current state. But it is definitely within our grasp because we have the potential to comprehend. By the simple practice of Guru Yoga, we can gain clarity, a purity of mind through our connection to the master's knowledge.

What the lama can show us is how to be free of our veils. The main method is meditation. It takes time to understand the essence of mind. And we need help. Needless to say, we have to go through the preparations, we have to work on ourselves. The good news is we can do it. Again, it goes back to the qualities we should nurture such as *depa*, *mögü* and *damtsik*. These qualities purify our mind and make room for deeper understanding. As a result, we will be able to connect with the authentic master and his realization. So the emphasis is to try to reach this point, it is achievable.

The main point of Dharma is to enable our mind to recognize the need to help others and to do so. After we receive the explanations from the lama, we apply them in practice. We work on improving our understanding by testing it out in daily life. Gradually, we become clearer about the meaning of the Dharma and we apply this understanding in assisting others.

Lay practitioners are not expected to give up everything living as a member of society. However, your attitudes are your own and they can be attuned to the Dharma. If you look, you will see that we are all inter-connected. Even if you work for yourself, the outcome will inevitably affect others as well. Take the examples of the connection between parents and children, teachers and students, and see how they influence one another. In the same way, we are influenced by the qualities of the master. When we participate in daily life at our level of understanding, we will in turn influence others. This is not to say we should feel proud. Rather, our attitude should be genuine and connected to the Dharma without any self-importance – this cannot be emphasized enough. By being sincere and natural in our contact with others, we are conveying the Dharma's message, and it is going to connect with people. We are then a messenger of the Dharma.

The caution is again the words sound simple. But if we think we are going to be like a teacher to others, then easily our pride will come up. For the same reason, outwardly we don't dress like a lama nor do we adopt a lama's mannerisms. This means just be ourselves as we are now and apply our understanding in our daily affairs. If you are a parent, then you can be like a lama to your children. *"Lama"* means someone who gives the right message and points to the proper directions. There are so many problems in our world created by wrong views and misguided communications. We cannot change the world, but we can change ourselves, our lives. This is why the Buddha taught to start with oneself. We prepare ourselves first. Learn properly from the authentic master who has received the transmissions from an authentic lineage. We will also naturally pass on the right message. In this way, we extend our help to those around us in difficult times and circumstances.

THE IMPORTANCE OF PRACTICE

When we try to be helpful to others, we will find that it is not so simple. We draw on the Dharma and Sangha for direction. We have to follow through with the entire process of receiving, reflecting, and practicing the teachings. We try to be clear about our experiences, ideas, and

thought processes. Ultimately, we purify the ignorance in our mind, the tendencies and disturbing emotions. Understanding through
words is not enough. This is why masters in the
past stressed the need to practice what we know.
Only then can real understanding take root in
us not just conceptually but naturally. We can
then work with the understanding through our
own seeing. When that happens, we no longer
need to ask what to do. The point is it takes
more than aspiration to change. It takes more
than sheer force to change. The point is it takes
practice to reach a real inner understanding so
that change occurs naturally from within.

Practice also offers another advantage – how
to deal with the disturbing emotions. At the moment, we may know how to seek temporary relief from them and to lessen the suffering. To
really understand the emotions and to work
with them effectively is very difficult. The way
to deal with emotions is not found in some intellectual or complex ideas but the solution
comes to us in a live experience quite spontaneously. Teachings can go into great lengths
about this subject but in practice, a simple answer can suddenly just appear. One example to
illustrate this point is the killing of mosquitoes.
You are told not to kill them. But until true compassion sets in, you don't want them around.
Even if you are a relatively kind person, you
can't help but slap the mosquito on your skin.
Compassion comes from a true understanding
of the nature of living things. When you have it,
you will not kill one mosquito, even if you are

told to. The same applies to the negative emotions of desire, pride, jealousy, anger, etc. We all know they cause suffering, but we still can't help being emotional. This means we don't yet see the point. We can't force the understanding either. It is not like replacing a battery in a flashlight and it will work. The answer has to come from our own understanding. And the Buddha said that this understanding has to come from meditation.

Meditation is a common word. Nowadays, there are so many different methods and applications of it. It is good to know the aim of Buddhist meditation. At the moment, we can see clearly, we can hear clearly, we can read clearly, yet somehow our understanding is blocked. We can't do what we want. Meditation aims at clearing up the blockages so we can function properly.

One way to help our children and friends is to give them correct information. For that to happen, we must get free of our inner disturbances because they make our minds unclear. When we are clear, we know what to do and say. But sometimes when we want something and obstacles are in our way, the disturbing emotions can arise. Again, we try to apply the Dharma teachings to get clearer about the situation. The more we practice doing this, the clearer we will be. The process is gradual. When we apply the teachings, try not to just grasp at the terms and concepts but the meanings behind the words. Don't get blocked by the Dharma ideas but go into their actual meanings to gain authentic understanding, the right understanding. It is only with this clear understanding that our communication with others will come across pure and natural. Then we will be authentic, too. The benefit is automatically there for ourselves and others. We don't have to wait until we are perfect to help others. The Dharma path is a live continuum where as we learn and make progress, we become naturally more effective and helpful to others. This is what it means to integrate the teachings in daily life. By practicing as much as we can in daily applications, our understanding will grow and our progress will be assured.

We always think that we have to force ourselves to practice. But actually, without the pressure to do it, we can do it. We can do the meditation to develop clarity in the mind. Especially in Vajrayana, practice is more than just sitting. We practice together with all the supports we have from our Refuge, our *yidam* and lama as already explained. Again, the strength of the supports depend on our inner conditions. Support means to connect to the Buddha, the *yidam*, the lineage masters and our lama, all who have perfect qualities. During the practice, we are in their presence. It is often said that we are inseparable from them and we meditate in this state. What is important is not how long we can meditate but our awareness. Whether we practice for ten minutes, thirty minutes, or a few hours, what matters is to remain aware and connected to the enlightened qualities. During meditation, staying connected through our

awareness is key just as being in the sun is necessary to achieve a tan. One difference between
meditation and getting a suntan is we don't
need to wait for a result in meditation and so
time does not matter.

The problem is our expectation for a result.
Even when it is not deliberate or obvious to us,
we are unconsciously expecting something. We
are happy when we get a sign like a certain appearance, or feeling. Such signs are not important. We must be aware that this type of
grasping is going on so we don't get stuck in our
tendencies.

We need to know that we have Buddha-nature, that we can receive the blessing. This confidence enables our mind to be inseparable from
the qualities of enlightenment. Our practice
then becomes spontaneous and natural. More
often than not, people think blessing is a feeling,
a vision, etc. But actually, the biographies of past
masters like Gampopa or Milarepa tell us that
blessing is not a feeling, that effects like feelings
are not so important. They can be positive, normal but not special. If we are not aware, we can
get caught up in such conditions. Seeing clearly
that everything is normal, we can move on
steadily and naturally.

Sometimes when we wish to be useful or
helpful, or we are trying to do our best, we run
into difficulties. We look to the teachings for
guidance, and we will find a method to resolve
the difficulties. "Method" here means a way of
clear understanding, a way of acting, and a way
of recognizing what is important. We don't go

along with our own projections. We need to relax so we can realize what is beneficial. This is the aim of Dharma coming through our application of it. It is perhaps difficult for us now given all our grasping and projections. Nevertheless, we try to understand little by little and gradually we will reach a clearer understanding.

Conclusion –
It All Depends on You

One cannot stress enough the importance of living every day grounded in the enlightened attitude because the benefits are enormous. *Bodhicitta* ushers positive merit into our mind stream that can fully ripen our mind's potential to become enlightened. Though not tangible, practically it enables us to function better. Positive karma results from a positive mind based in the enlightened attitude. In other words, *bodhicitta* directly influences karma. This is why the teachings always emphasize the generating of *bodhicitta*. At the same time, it is not something new that we have to acquire or learn, rather, we have the potential to develop it. And we have to be introduced to it because we don't understand it properly. It is really our own capacity. The word, *bodhicitta*, may sound "fantastic" so we are not quite sure what to do or we may feel confused. If so, simply think of it as a positive influence or a good condition. We tend to think that if only the external conditions were good, then things would work out and we'd be healthy, happy, and well. However, it is really our inner attitudes that sets the tone of situations outside of us. When our mind is polluted or negative, things turn out not so smooth and they seem more of a burden to us. And vice versa, when our mind is positive, then the externals are likewise favorable.

The positive attitude actually comes from a level of awareness in the mind. When we hold all living beings as important and as equal as ourselves, it exerts a positive influence in us. The understanding of equality of all beings comes from merit, which enables us to be always helpful and useful to others even in very small ways. Whatever good we generate, we don't keep it for ourselves but dedicate it again towards the benefit of everyone. Even if we cannot be fully dedicated to others, we can at least recognize the opportunities to do good when they appear so we can then choose to act accordingly. Up until now, we have not been aware of how things are and what they mean. Once we understand, we will see more precisely as to how to act in a way that is beneficial to others. Through our positive actions, we will accumulate merit. Positive actions always follow positive thinking. And positive thinking means to benefit not just a few people but everyone without exception. And it takes a precise understanding of the conditions of beings which will enable us to act spontaneously in a positive way.

To get the precise understanding, we

progress through a standard way of learning. It goes from listening to the meaning first, then to reflecting and thinking about the meaning, and then to act according to the meaning. The result is greater clarity of mind. In this way, we can ripen our inner potential that is already there allowing us ever greater understanding, a precise understanding of the conditions of beings so we can help them.

We can test the validity of the Dharma in our daily situations. We should not feel we have to act out of obligation, or to serve out a court sentence, or to act out of self-interest only. When we apply the meaning of *bodhicitta*, we will find that it means that everyone is equal in the sense that we are all subject to the same conditions, which is not how we perceive others right now.

With *bodhicitta* in mind, we try to be useful in practical situations. For instance, when someone approaches us for help, we tend to evaluate the situation to see if the help is warranted. If we find the other is better off than we are, there is a tendency to refuse. That kind of feeling can appear, or we might feel that we don't want to help. Of course, we should not force ourselves either. Rather, we can try to respond in whatever way we can. Even a very small help can afford the person a feeling of support or reprieve. To try to be more open is very necessary to really appreciate the meaning of *bodhicitta*. Through reflection, we will see more precisely our own motivation. It wakes us up and we may discover that our attitude is in fact negative: *"I don't want to do it; or I don't feel good; or I can't do it."* These thoughts may arise yet they are not important. Just let them pass and try to see what really matters in a certain situation. It might simplify or clarify the difficulty or complication for us. The answer will become evident and we will know what to do. We don't necessarily go looking to help others or not to help. We don't need to decide ahead of time either. Within a given situation, we will see through our momentary thoughts our attitudes or states of mind. Gradually, with practice, we will begin to understand the "equality" in all sentient beings. It is crucial that we discover this by our own experience.

A clear mind properly oriented in *bodhicitta* makes us grounded and stable. It is because when we clearly understand how things are, and not just superficially, we are no longer confused, distracted, or helpless. This is one result of wisdom. Wisdom does not mean a quiet mind. It is a very clear mind understanding everything. Since the mind is very clear, it cannot be distracted. This means less suffering already. Until Buddhahood is reached, there will appear different kinds of suffering yet they will not block us as mind's clarity or wisdom develops. To achieve this kind of result, we must be earnestly rooted in enlightened attitude throughout the path. We practice meditation and the application of *bodhicitta* regularly. Gradually, the results will come.

We must make use of all the opportunities, circumstances, and our relationships with people along our way. We reflect, we apply what we know, and we really try to engage in the *bod-hicitta* attitude. Little by little, our understanding will increase and we will become clearer. Then, accordingly, our capacity to help others will increase. Without a proper understanding, even if we wish to help now, we don't really know how, and our emotions always get in the way. Therefore, right here and now, we make real efforts to develop our capabilities. We don't have to be in solitude to develop clarity. If our efforts and actions are properly motivated, our conditions will improve: our merit accumulation, the conditions of our mind, and our comprehension during Dharma lectures. Everything will make more sense, and we become more comfortable with ourselves. Our mind is peaceful, joyful, and we are ready to work for others. When we do, we gain more merit which will further strengthen our capacity to understand and help.

Right now, you may question whether the enlightened attitude is really all that important. The resistance fluctuates, sometimes strong, at times weak. When it arises, reflect on the essential meaning of *bodhicitta* and your state of mind. Ask yourself which takes priority. This will help to clear the mind so you can work with the situation at hand. Otherwise, you will feel that you can't do it, or you feel pressured to act in a certain way. But if you reflect, the answer is there even if you are unable to carry it out. Over time, you will one day be able to act as you see fit. This does not require you to abandon your habitual ways. They will naturally ad-

just and change according to the insights you un-
cover. This is why it is so important to reflect,
to really see the truth of things. It is the only way
to break free of habits and concepts, a rigid mental system that brings us much suffering. It is not
so easy to uphold your daily life situations to the
standards of *bodhicitta*. But through consistent
effort and practice, you will gradually be able to
work with it.

Some people misunderstand the meaning of
"obscuration due to knowledge." They think
knowledge is to be avoided which is not the case
at all. It is just that we are not able to work with
what we have learnt. This is an important point
for reflection. It will clear up a lot of confusion.
You may learn the skills and knowledge to be a
philosopher, an architect, a doctor, or an engi-
neer. You are very involved in your own field of
expertise but you should be careful that your
specialty does not block you or narrow your
point of view. In other words, you should keep
knowledge in perspective.

A clear mind does not complicate things. It
does not bring harmful or confusing results. But
a clear mind can only come about through careful reflection. You are all individually educated
with a good store of knowledge. But you still feel
there's more. By careful examination, you will
inevitably discover that what is missing is the
truth. This is the reason why some people look
to Buddhism. The truth is not a foreign external
thing. Look within yourself and you will find it.
Apply the Dharma in daily life situations. From
your interactions with others, you hone your

understanding and it will enable you to act with wisdom. The development of wisdom is gradual and not easy but nevertheless important.

A practitioner is someone who practices meditation regularly in order to understand Buddha-nature. The understanding is on a different level that can clear away the illusions or ignorance, gain wisdom and achieve enlightened mind. Many people do long retreats to accomplish this ultimate result. The methods are the practice of compassion, Guru Yoga, or any of the *yidam* practices. When we prepare by properly engaging in these practices, the results will happen naturally. We have to put in the effort. We cannot wait for the result to happen to us so we follow the practice instructions. However, when we are in the actual practice, there is another understanding. This story about His Holiness Karmapa's meeting with an Indian teacher may illustrate the point.

In 1972, I went with His Holiness Karmapa on a pilgrimage in India. We visited Bodhgaya and other holy places in southern India. In Bombay, the Karmapa received and accepted an invitation from a well-known Indian Hindu teacher. We went to his ashram in a little village called Ganeshspur. There were many people who came for teachings. During a break, the Karmapa and the Indian teacher were together in a room with some disciples. They were chatting casually when the Indian teacher asked the Karmapa, "Can you show us one miracle?" In India, miracles are considered very important because they show the achievement of mind. In ancient time, the great masters such as Tilopa and Naropa were able to express their knowledge of mind by performing miracles. The Karmapa replied, "Not today, but tomorrow during the crown ceremony." Everyone was quiet. The thirty of us who were in the Karmapa's entourage thought that surely the next day would show something special!

The next day, the crown ceremony took place for six hundred people, the majority of whom were Indians. We were all paying attention but for us nothing happened other than the usual rites that were performed for the ceremony. But afterwards, the Indian teacher who sat there like the rest of us, was fully convinced of His Holiness' realization. For him, something did happen during the ceremony, which made him believe that the Karmapa had attained the most important achievement in the Hindu religion – enlightenment.

This story shows that to get the precise meaning really depends on an individual's own capacity. The crown ceremony is profound in that it introduces us to the realization of mind. But in order for this to happen, each of us has to gather all the required conditions and accomplish all the necessary preparations. Again, this means that the practitioner always receives from the teacher the meaning exactly according to his own capacity. Some people can become realized after receiving the teachings while it takes time for others. This also illustrates the point that miracles and fantasies are not important. What is important is that we get down to work on ourselves. We put in the effort so that our own inner potential may ripen. Just as Naropa could not find the teacher when he had not done the proper preparations, we will not realize the truth until we do the work and practices.

All the teachings and explanations are very important. We may sometimes feel that we will experience something very special. But then, everything just goes along in an ordinary way. Meeting a great teacher will not give us anything. Naropa looked all over to find Tilopa when the latter was there following him. Very skillfully, Tilopa introduced Naropa to the recognition of the important points such as *bodhicitta* and devotion. Tilopa showed Naropa that running after a teacher did not produce any realization. Realization has to come from within through inner reflection, by applying the teachings, and integrating the teachings into our understanding.

It all comes back to our own preparations and to our own efforts. Due to our illusions, we try to be or act in a certain way but we never really get the precise point. To get the precise point requires the right preparation. We don't necessarily have to go through complex and difficult situations. On the contrary, if we are practicing and preparing ourselves properly, then through very simple and ordinary situations, we will understand quite precisely and naturally the meanings. All the Vajrayana teachings agree on this point. There may be great and profound terms, but if you try to grasp at them you will miss the essential meanings. Some people find the Dharma teachings ineffective because they have not done the groundwork. We begin with the enlightened attitude because it can clarify everything so that we will understand all the meanings of the Dharma teachings, apply the teachings in our lives and gradually open ourselves to the real and profound understanding that is wisdom.

Index of Tibetan Terms

The Tibetan terms in this index follow closely the standard phonetic established by the researchers and linguists of the Tibetan and Himalayan Library (www.thlib.org). The Wylie transliteration are without diacritics.

The following translations follow Lama Jigme Rinpoche's explanations in this book. Some terms may have a different meaning in a different context.

Dzokrim	*rdzogs rim*	Completion phase
Gendun	*dge 'dun*	Virtuous community
Gom	*sgom*	To meditate, to familiarize oneself with
Gyu	*rgyu*	Cause
Gyurwa	*bsgyur ba*	To change
Jinlap	*sbyin rlabs*	Blessing
Kyerim	*skyed rim*	Creation phase
Lama	bla ma	Teacher
Lamé neljor	*bla ma'i rnal 'byor*	Guru yoga
Le	*las*	Action, karma
Lojong	*blo sbyong*	Mind-training
Lung	*lung*	Ritual reading
Marikpa	*ma rig pa*	Ignorance
Men ngak	*man ngag*	Expression of individual realization
Mögü	*mos gus*	Trust and devotion
Nepa	*gnas pa*	To rest
Ngepa	*nges pa*	Certainty
Nyönmong	*nyon mongs*	Emotion, affliction
Rikpa	*rig pa*	Clear awareness
Sam	*bsam*	To reflect, to contemplate
Sangye	*sangs rgyas*	Buddha
Semchen	*sems can*	Sentient being
Shezhin	*shes bzhin*	Mindful awareness
Tö	*thos*	To listen
Tri	*khrid*	Instruction/ Explanation of practice
Tsok	*tshogs*	Offering feast
Wang	*dbang*	Empowerment, initiation
Yeshe	*ye shes*	Wisdom
Yidam	*yid dam*	*Yidam*
Zhine	*zhi gnas*	Calm abiding

Publishing finished
by CPI, Firmin Didot
Au Mesnil-sur-l'Estrée

Number of publisher : 0009
Legal deposit : November 2012
Number of printing : 115453

Printed in France